COMMONSENSE
ARCHITECTURE

COMMONSENSE
ARCHITECTURE

A CROSS-CULTURAL SURVEY OF PRACTICAL DESIGN PRINCIPLES

JOHN S. TAYLOR

W·W·NORTON & COMPANY
New York   London

Published simultaneously in Canada by Penguin Books Canada Ltd,
2801 John Street, Markham, Ontario L3R 1B4
Printed in the United States of America

First published as a Norton paperback 1986

Library of Congress Cataloging in Publication Data
Taylor, John S.
  Commonsense Architecture
  1. Vernacular Architecture.   I. Title.
NA208.T39   1983   720   82–14522

ISBN 0-393-30330-6

W. W. Norton & Company, Inc., 500 Fifth Avenue, New York, N. Y. 10110
W. W. Norton & Company Ltd., 37 Great Russell Street, London WC1B 3NU

 2 3 4 5 6 7 8 9 0

I AM ESPECIALLY GRATEFUL FOR THE ASSISTANCE OF NITA LESCHER, JIM MAIRS, JANET BYRNE, CLEE AND SUZANNE EDGAR, ETSUKO PENNER, THE GOVERNMENT OF JAPAN, AND PAN AMERICAN AIRWAYS, FOR THE SUPPORT FROM ALL MY FAMILY AND FRIENDS, AND MOST IMPORTANTLY, FOR THE PRAGMATIC SPIRIT OF HISTORY'S ANONYMOUS BUILDERS.

Contents

Introduction

"WHEN ONE HAS COMPLETED THE NECESSARY ... ONE IMMEDIATELY COMES UPON THE BEAUTIFUL AND THE PLEASING."

VOLTAIRE

THE STRAIGHTFORWARD RESPONSE TO BOTH HUMAN NEEDS AND ENVIRONMENTAL FORCES GIVES FOLK HOUSES OF THE WORLD A REFRESHING QUALITY. THEIR BEAUTY LIES IN THE STRONG LINK BETWEEN FORM AND PURPOSE AND IN THE ABSENCE OF COSMETICS OR REDUNDANCY.

A SCARCITY OF RESOURCES LED HISTORY'S ANONYMOUS BUILDERS TO ACHIEVE A HIGHLY ECONOMICAL AND PRACTICAL FORM OF UNSELFCONSCIOUS ARCHITECTURE ROOTED IN TIMELESS PRINCIPLES OF REASON RATHER THAN IN TEMPORARY FASHIONS OR WHIMS.

ALONG WITH MANY BENEFITS, ADVANCED TECHNOLOGY HAS ALLOWED US TO BE IMPRACTICAL, WITH THE KNOWLEDGE THAT ARTIFICIAL MEANS ARE AVAILABLE TO OVERCOME INEFFICIENCY. RECENT SHORTAGES OF CAPITAL AND ENERGY RESOURCES SHOULD FORCE US TO RECOGNIZE THAT PRACTICALITY MUST BE AN ESSENTIAL ELEMENT IN CONTEMPORARY ARCHITECTURE. IN THIS RESPECT VERNACULAR FOLK ARCHITECTURE CAN TEACH US A GREAT DEAL.

COMMONSENSE ARCHITECTURE DEPICTS INDIGENOUS ARCHITECTURE'S RESPONSIVENESS TO HUMAN NEEDS AND TO THE ENVIRONMENT, WITH EXAMPLES FROM ALL PARTS OF THE WORLD. THE BOOK IS NOT A TREATISE AGAINST TECHNOLOGY, BUT RATHER A CATALOGUE OF COMMONSENSE PRINCIPLES THAT CAN HELP US USE TECHNOLOGY AS AN EFFICIENT TOOL INSTEAD OF AS A CLOAK FOR INEFFICIENT DESIGNS.

THE FIRST SECTION ILLUSTRATES HOW BUILDINGS RESPOND TO EXTERNAL ENVIRONMENTAL FACTORS SUCH AS CLIMATE AND PREDATORS. THE SECOND SECTION DESCRIBES WAYS IN WHICH VARIOUS ACTIVITIES SUCH AS SLEEPING AND COOKING ARE ACCOMMODATED WITHIN DWELLINGS. AND THE FINAL SECTION INVESTIGATES THE MATERIALS AND CONSTRUCTION PRACTICES USED TO BUILD SHELTERS. TO MAINTAIN A PURELY FUNCTIONAL APPROACH TO FOLK ARCHITECTURE, CERTAIN CULTURAL INFLUENCES — RELIGION AND POLITICS, FOR EXAMPLE — HAVE NOT BEEN DISCUSSED. IT SHOULD BE NOTED, HOWEVER, THAT MOST OF THESE TRADITIONS HAVE A RATIONAL, UTILITARIAN BASIS. TO INSURE THEIR CONTINUED USE, THESE IDEAS HAVE GRADUALLY BEEN INCORPORATED INTO THE CULTURAL LORE THAT GUIDES BUILDERS. IN SOME CASES A PRACTICE MAY THRIVE EVEN AFTER THE REASON FOR IT HAS BEEN FORGOTTEN.

COMMONSENSE ARCHITECTURE WAS CREATED IN THE HOPE THAT THE WISDOM THAT SHAPED THE VERNACULAR ARCHITECTURE OF THE PAST WILL HELP US REDUCE OUR DEPENDENCE ON RESOURCES BY REVIVING OUR USE OF RESOURCEFULNESS.

SECTION I - PROTECTION FROM THE ENVIRONMENT

NATURE AS PROVIDER OF SHELTER

SHELTERS EVOLVED TO GIVE PROTECTION FROM THE HOSTILE ASPECTS OF THE ENVIRONMENT, PRIMARILY HARSH WEATHER AND THREATS FROM OTHER ANIMALS. FOR EONS TREE-DWELLING APES HAVE CONSTRUCTED CRUDE LEAF AND TWIG PLATFORMS IN THE TREES TO RAISE THEMSELVES ABOVE THE DANGERS ON THE GROUND AND TO PARTIALLY WARD OFF THE RAIN AND HOT SUN.

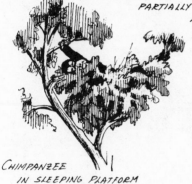

CHIMPANZEE
IN SLEEPING PLATFORM

ARBOREAL
JUNGLE TENT
USED IN A BIOLOGICAL
RESEARCH PROGRAM
AMAZON JUNGLE, 1980

PEOPLE HAVE CONTINUED
THIS PRACTICE OF
RISING ABOVE DANGERS
BY CONSTRUCTING
AERIE FORTRESSES.

METÉORA, GREECE

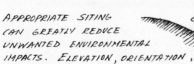

APPROPRIATE SITING CAN GREATLY REDUCE UNWANTED ENVIRONMENTAL IMPACTS. ELEVATION, ORIENTATION, AND WIND PROTECTION ARE CAREFULLY CONSIDERED BY BOTH ANIMALS AND TRADITIONAL INDIGENOUS BUILDERS.

Most primitive dwellings show a strong sensitivity to local conditions. Out of necessity they take maximum advantage of the natural amenities to gain increased comfort and protection.

Cliff Dwellings Mesa Verde, Colorado

Shelter built under a projecting boulder Portugal

Where conditions were right, builders often chose to create shelters by carving them out of the earth.

Dwellings partly cut into cliffs and partly built out from them Setenil, Spain

Elaborate facades were added to many dwellings carved out of soft stone cliffs. Touraine, France

FOR MILLIONS OF YEARS MANY ANIMALS
HAVE USED UNDERGROUND SANCTUARIES
FOR PROTECTION FROM COLD, HEAT, RAIN,
SNOW, PREDATORS, ETC. EARLY MAN
LEARNED A GREAT DEAL ABOUT
SHELTERS FROM THE OTHER ANIMALS
AND SAW THE
VALUE OF THE
BURROWED
HOME.

SMALL ANT COLONY

DWELLINGS
HOLLOWED OUT
OF NATURAL CONES
OF POROUS LIMESTONE,
OR TUFA.

CAPPADOCIA, TURKEY

NORTH

FRONT VIEW AND PLAN OF HOUSES CUT
OUT OF A VOLCANIC STONE, CALLED TUFF, IN MASSAFRA,
ITALY. THE FAN-SHAPED ROOMS
LEFT A MINIMAL HOLE IN THE
FACE OF THE FRAGILE ROCK
AND HAD NO DARK
CORNERS.

HOUSE DUG INTO ROCK
CONE COMPLETE WITH
A FINISHED FACADE
AND A CHIMNEY

GUADIX, SPAIN

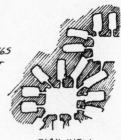

DWELLINGS DUG OUT OF SOFT LOESS SOIL AND RADIATING FROM A SUNKEN CENTRAL COURT (NORTHERN CHINA)

PLAN VIEW

THE SUNKEN COURT CONCEPT IS STILL USED EFFECTIVELY TODAY.

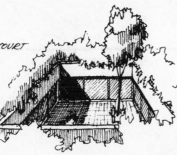

JOHN BARNARD'S ECOLOGY HOUSE OSTERVILLE, MASSACHUSETTS

SOME EARTH-SHELTERED HOMES ARE DUG INTO A HILL SO THAT ONLY ONE WALL (USUALLY TO THE SOUTH) IS EXPOSED FOR ACCESS AND LIGHT.

BANKED HOUSE, AMERICAN MIDWEST

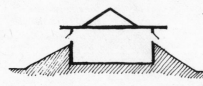

IN HIS COOP HOMESTEAD PLANS IN 1942, FRANK LLOYD WRIGHT PROPOSED SHELTERING THE HOUSE WITH AN EARTH BERM.

STAYING DRY

OFFERING PROTECTION
FROM THE RAIN IS A
PRIMARY GOAL FOR
SHELTERS IN MOST
CLIMATES.

HUT ON ALOR ISLAND
NEAR BORNEO
THIS SIMPLE SHELTER
SERVES AS BOTH A RAIN
HAT AND SUN SHADE.

HOUSE ON FLORES ISLAND
THE STEEP THATCH ROOF IS
DESIGNED TO SHED THE
HEAVY INDONESIAN
RAINS.

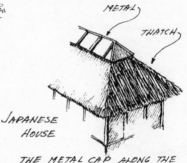

METAL

THATCH

JAPANESE
HOUSE

THE METAL CAP ALONG THE
PEAK OF THE ROOF PROTECTS
THIS OFTEN LEAKY SPOT IN
THATCH ROOFS.

HAY STORAGE
SHED, HOLLAND

AS HAY IS ADDED
THE ROOF IS RAISED WITH ROPES
FROM THE POLES. THE ROOF
SHEDS THE RAIN, WHILE AIR
CAN STILL GET IN TO DRY
THE HAY.

EARLY GREEK
HOUSE

COVERED
INTERIOR BALCONIES
CREATE LIVING SPACES OUT OF THE SUN AND RAIN.

THE SMALL HIP SEGMENT ON
THIS GABLE ROOF PROTECTS
A SMALL PORCH THAT
CAN BE USED IN ALL
WEATHER AS A PLACE TO
WORK AND TO DRY FOOD
AND CLOTHES.

COVERED PORCH
ON LAKE GENEVA, SWITZERLAND

THIS HOUSE IN NORTHWEST
NEW GUINEA NOT ONLY GIVES
GOOD PROTECTION FROM THE
HEAVY RAINS BUT ALSO
INSURES COOLING
THROUGH-VENTILATION.

KAMBOT HOUSE
SEPIK, NORTHWEST NEW GUINEA

SMALL ROOFS, HOODS,
AND CANTILEVERED
OVERHANGS ARE
ALSO VERY
EFFECTIVE DEVICES
FOR DIVERTING
THE RAIN.

DOOR HOOD ON
PENNSYLVANIA
FARMHOUSE

PENTICE, OR PENT ROOF,
ON A BARN IN
PENNSYLVANIA

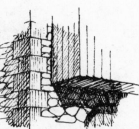

CANTILEVERED
OUTSHOT ON
BARN IN
DELAWARE

HERE THE OVER-
HANGING UPPER
FLOOR ACTS AS
A RAIN HOOD
FOR LOWER LEVEL.

IN AREAS WHERE FRESH WATER WAS
A VERY LIMITED COMMODITY MANY
INNOVATIVE SYSTEMS EVOLVED FOR
THE COLLECTION AND STORAGE
OF RAINWATER.

FIELD SHELTER
SOUTHERN ITALY

THE FLAT ROOF IS USED FOR
DRYING CROPS AND THE PLASTER DOWNSPOUT
CARRIES RAINWATER TO A CISTERN (1600)

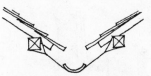

GUTTERS AND DOWNSPOUTS ARE
THE MAIN TOOLS FOR
WATER COLLECTION:

JAPANESE SLUNG BAMBOO
GUTTER SERVING TWO ROOFS

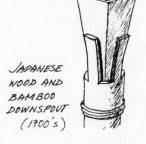

JAPANESE
WOOD AND
BAMBOO
DOWNSPOUT
(1700's)

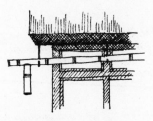

JAPANESE BAMBOO
GUTTER AND DOWNSPOUT
HUNG FROM METAL
BRACKETS
(1659)

LOG GUTTER
FORT CLATSOP,
OREGON
(1805)

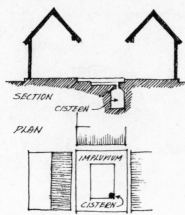

BENIN HOUSE
SOUTHERN NIGERIA

THE CENTRAL COURT-
YARD, OR IMPLUVIUM,
ACTS AS A RAINWATER
COLLECTION BASIN THAT
EMPTIES INTO A CISTERN
BURRIED AT ONE
CORNER.

SECTION

CISTERN

PLAN

IMPLUVIUM

CISTERN

THE STONE TRULLO
DWELLINGS IN APULIA,
ITALY OFTEN HAVE
DOWNSPOUTS THAT CARRY
RAINWATER INTO LARGE, ROOFED
CISTERNS. THIS WATER IS
USED BOTH FOR DRINKING
AND FOR WATERING
CROPS.

LIVING
SPACE

CISTERN

IN THE AMERICAN WEST, THE
CUSTOMARY WATER BARREL WAS A
AN ABOVE-GROUND CISTERN
FOR RAINWATER.

PUEBLO DWELLING
ROOF

SCUPPER

SUDDEN RAINS
IN THE AMERICAN
SOUTHWEST ARE
QUICKLY DRAINED
FROM THE FLAT EARTH
ROOFS BY SCUPPERS THAT
USUALLY DIRECT THE WATER INTO BARRELS.

LIVING SPACE

18

SIDE VIEW

CZECHOSLOVAKIAN HOUSE
THE GABLE WALL IS
PROTECTED BY A ROOF
PROJECTION AND A
CANTILEVERED, OR
JETTIED, SECOND FLOOR.

PROTECTING THE WALLS OF
THE HOUSE FROM THE RAIN
IS IMPORTANT FOR THEIR PRE-
SERVATION, AND VARIOUS
DESIGN ELEMENTS HAVE
EVOLVED TO MEET
THIS NEED.

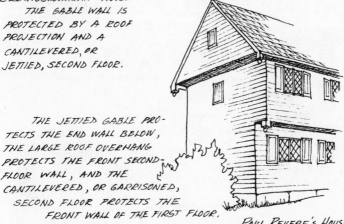

THE JETTIED GABLE PRO-
TECTS THE END WALL BELOW,
THE LARGE ROOF OVERHANG
PROTECTS THE FRONT SECOND-
FLOOR WALL, AND THE
CANTILEVERED, OR GARRISONED,
SECOND FLOOR PROTECTS THE
FRONT WALL OF THE FIRST FLOOR.

PAUL REVERE'S HOUSE
BOSTON, MASSACHUSETTS
(BUILT IN 1660)

MEXICAN HOUSE
NEAR HIDALGO
THE FANNED GABLE OF
HAND-SPLIT SHAKES PROTECTS
THE SOFT MUD BRICK
WALL BELOW.

COTTAGE
CAMBRIDGESHIRE, ENGLAND
THE SLOPING PENTICE
BOARDS PROTECT THE GABLE WALL.

SIFNOS ISLAND, GREECE

PLASTER OVER THESE ROUGH STONE WALLS PROTECTS THE SOFT MASONRY.

MASONRY WALLS ARE PARTICULARLY VULNERABLE TO DETERIORATION WHEN EXPOSED TO MOISTURE, SO THEY REQUIRE SPECIAL PROTECTION.

FIELD WALL, GREECE
THE PLASTER CAP PROTECTS THE STONEWORK BELOW.

PARAPET WALL, MEXICO

SLOPING TILES KEEP THE RAIN FROM EATING AWAY THE SOFT MUD BRICK WALLS.

MEDIEVAL WINDOW ENGLAND

THE DRIP BAND AROUND THE UPPER SIDE OF THE WINDOW PREVENTS WATER FROM FLOWING DOWN THE WALL AND INTO THE SASH AND SILL JOINTS.

DRIP COURSE ENGLAND

THE PROJECTING COURSE OF BRICKS KEEPS WATER FROM FLOWING DOWN THE WALL AND DAMAGING THE MASONRY.

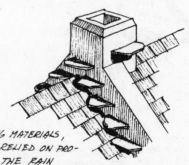

LACKING MODERN FLASHING MATERIALS, EARLY BUILDERS IN WALES RELIED ON PROJECTING SLATES TO KEEP THE RAIN AWAY FROM THE ROOF / WALL JUNCTION.

PROJECTING LOGGIA, ST. AUGUSTINE, FLORIDA (1700's)

THE SLOPED FLOOR PREVENTS STANDING WATER FROM ROTTING THE FLOOR.

BANNISTER JOINT, ST. AUGUSTINE, FLORIDA (1700's)

THE V-JOINT KEEPS WATER FROM COLLECTING IN THE JOINT AND ROTTING THE WOOD.

PORCH POST, VIRGINIA (1800's)

THE METAL BASE PROTECTS THE POST FROM WATER THAT RUNS OFF THE PORCH.

STONE SCUPPERS KEEP THE WATER OFF THE PLASTERED WALLS OF THE STONE TRULLO.

STONE TRULLO APULIA, ITALY (1600's)

JAPANESE GUTTER AND DOWNSPOUT

THE WATER FLOWS ALONG THE CHAINS TO THE GRAVEL BED BELOW AND DOESN'T SPLASH THE HOUSE WALL.

GRAVEL BED

JAPANESE FENCE POST (1600's)

THE BASE IS STONE TO RESIST ROT AND THE UPPER PART IS WOOD.

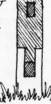

PARASOL ROOF
WITHOUT WALLS,
SAMOA

IF WATER VAPOR IS ALLOWED TO
CONDENSE ON WOOD OR OTHER
PLANT BUILDING MATERIALS IT
WILL CAUSE MILDEW AND ROT.
A VARIETY OF TECHNIQUES
CAN PREVENT THIS.

IN HOT, HUMID AREAS IT IS
IMPORTANT TO PROMOTE GOOD
FLOW-THROUGH VENTILATION
TO PREVENT
CONDENSATION.

OPEN REED WALL,
MADAGASCAR

ALPINE BARN
(1818)

AS MOIST AIR PASSES
THROUGH A WALL FROM
THE WARM SIDE TO THE
COLD SIDE, IT MAY REACH
ITS DEW POINT AND CON-
DENSE WITHIN THE WALL,
CAUSING MILDEW AND ROT.
VAPOR BARRIERS IN
MODERN HOMES ARE IN-
STALLED TO STOP THE
MOISTURE BEFORE IT
GETS INTO THE WALL.

THE OPEN CONSTRUCTION OF
THE EXTERIOR HAY MOW PRO-
TECTED BY THE DEEP ROOF
OVERHANG ALLOWS FOR AIR
FLOW TO DRY THE HAY.

WALL SECTION:

ROT CAUSED BY
CONDENSATION IN A
COOL, MOIST CRAWL-
SPACE IS CURBED
WITH FOUNDATION
VENTS.

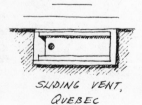

SLIDING VENT,
QUEBEC

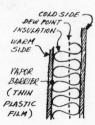

COLD SIDE
DEW POINT
INSULATION
WARM
SIDE
VAPOR
BARRIER
(THIN
PLASTIC
FILM)

PROTECTION FROM THE WIND

HOUSE FORMS THAT OFFER LITTLE AIR
RESISTANCE AND CREATE NO TURBULENCE
REDUCE THE STRUCTURAL AND
THERMAL IMPACTS OF
THE WIND.

WIND

WIND OVER THE
RECTANGULAR HOUSE
CREATES TURBULENT EDDIES,
WHILE THE WIND FLOWS EVENLY OVER
THE SEMICIRCULAR ONE.

WIND

THE HOUSE BELOW HAS
A ROOF SHAPED LIKE A BOAT'S
HULL THAT HAS ITS BOW
TURNED INTO THE WIND.

LEAN-TO WIND SHELTER
AKSEHIR, TURKEY

WIND

NORMANDY FARMHOUSE

THE SALTBOX HOUSES OF NEW
ENGLAND LET THE COLD NORTH
WINDS GLIDE OVER THE LONG,
SLOPING ROOF.

NEW ENGLAND SALTBOX
(1800's)

THE TERRAIN AROUND
THIS CONTEMPORARY
EARTH-SHELTERED HOME
IS CONTOURED TO CREATE A MINIMUM
OF AIR TURBULENCE.

THE BACKSTRIP BY THIS ARAB
TENT BREAKS THE HOT,
SANDY DESERT WINDS.

INUIT IGLOOS
OFTEN HAD A WIND-
SCREEN WALL BY THE
ENTRANCE

ROCKY MOUNTAIN
TEPEE WITH
WIND SCREEN

EARLY JAPANESE BUILDERS
OFTEN PLACED STONES
ON THE WOOD SHINGLES
TO PREVENT THE WIND
FROM BLOWING THEM OFF.

IN IRELAND, A ROPE NET WEIGHTED WITH
STONES SECURES THE THATCH.

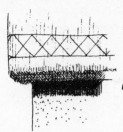

THIS ROPE BAND KEEPS THE
WIND FROM PULLING UP THE
EDGE OF THE THATCH ROOF.

SUSSEX, ENGLAND
(1699)

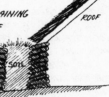

RAIN DRAINING
OFF THE ROOF
COMPACTS THE SOIL
IN THE WALL TO MAKE
THE HOUSE MORE RE-
SISTANT TO THE
WIND.

BLACK HOUSE
HEBRIDES, SCOTLAND

A)

WIND →

B)

WIND →

WIND PRESSURE ON AN
UNBRACED FRAME (A) CAN
PUSH IT OVER, BUT
DIAGONAL BRACING
AT THE CORNERS (B) WILL FORM
RIGID JOINTS THAT CAN
RESIST THE LATERAL FORCE.

THE DIAGONAL BRACES ON THE
CORNER OF THIS BUILDING HELP IT
RESIST THE LATERAL
WIND PRESSURE.

HRONSEK,
CZECHOSLOVAKIA

FOUR MASSIVE
EXTERNAL SOLID MASONRY
BUTTRESSES BRACE THIS
BUILDING IN FRANCE AGAINST
THE WIND.

Staying Warm

The earliest human settlements were centered in subtropical regions that had adequate food and water resources and arable land. As settlements spread to the more temperate regions, the problem of staying warm during the winter became critical. Caves offered limited protection, but as civilization grew, more successful ways of dealing with the cold were found.

The choice of the dwelling site was very important. The intention was to maximize the natural advantages of the site — such as terrain, geology, hydrology, vegetation, etc. — and minimize the impact of the cold.

The Anasazi Indians at Mesa Verde built their dwellings into rock cliffs. These niches faced south for the warming sun and gave sanctuary from the cold winds.

Balcony House
Mesa Verde, Colorado
13th Century

Hill Dwellings, Pakistan

In the mountains of Pakistan the people build their houses on steep, south-facing slopes to give shelter on the north and to capture the sun's warmth. This practice also leaves the entire river valley free for cultivation.

ANOTHER VERY EFFECTIVE WAY TO REDUCE
A DWELLING'S EXPOSURE TO THE COLD IS TO USE
BUILDING SHAPES THAT MAXIMIZE THE SPACE CONTAINED
WHILE MINIMIZING THE EXPOSED SURFACE AREA.

SPHERE
VOLUME = 36 UNITS^3
SURFACE AREA = 52.7 UNITS^2
VOLUME / SURFACE AREA RATIO = .68

OVENBIRD NEST

HEMISPHERE
VOLUME = 36 UNITS^3
SURFACE AREA = 62.78 UNITS^2
VOLUME / SURFACE AREA RATIO = .57

INUIT IGLOO

CUBE
VOLUME = 36 UNITS^3
SURFACE AREA = 65.4 UNITS^2
VOLUME / SURFACE AREA RATIO = .55

CANADIAN LOG CABIN

RECTANGULAR SOLID
VOLUME = 36 UNITS^3
SURFACE AREA = 96 UNITS^2
VOLUME / SURFACE AREA RATIO = .38

CONTEMPORARY
HAWAIIAN HOUSE

BY CLUSTERING MANY
DWELLING UNITS IN A
SINGLE MASS, THE
EXPOSED SURFACE
AREA CAN BE
SIGNIFICANTLY
REDUCED.

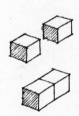

ACOMA PUEBLO
NEW MEXICO

SOME BEES AND WASPS USE
HEXAGONAL TUBES IN HIVE
BUILDING. THIS SHAPE ENCLOSES
A GOOD DEAL OF VOLUME AND
ALLOWS TIGHT PACKING OF THE
MODULES FOR MINIMUM EXPOSURE.

SECTION OF
HONEYBEE HIVE

A SIMPLE, EFFECTIVE, AND LOW-COST WAY IN WHICH TO REDUCE THE IMPACT OF THE COLD IS TO USE THE EARTH TO TEMPER THE HOUSE.
SLIGHTLY BELOW THE FROST LINE SOIL WILL REMAIN AT ABOUT 50° F. YEAR-ROUND.

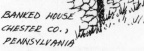

BANKED HOUSE CHESTER CO., PENNSYLVANIA
BY BUILDING INTO A SLOPE THE LOWER FLOOR IS PROTECTED BY EARTH ON THREE SIDES.

TEMPORARY MOUNTAIN SHELTER, PAKISTAN — EARTH AND ROCKS ARE PILED UP AROUND PART OF THE STRUCTURE.

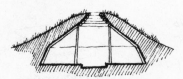

ESKIMO EARTH-SHELTERED DWELLING, CANADA — EARTH COVERS BOTH WALLS AND ROOF.

FARMHOUSE NORTHERN ICELAND — BUILT INTO HILLS WITH EARTH SHIELDING THE ROOF AND WALLS

LOG-END CAVE HOUSE, WEST CHAZY, NEW YORK — ONLY ONE WALL IS EXPOSED, WHILE EARTH PROTECTS THE REST OF THE HOUSE.

WHERE GEOLOGICAL CONDITIONS WERE
FAVORABLE, MANY BUILDERS CHOSE TO
COMPLETELY SHELTER THEMSELVES WITH
THE LAND BY DIGGING INTO IT.
THESE TROGLODYTE DWELLINGS
BECAME VERY ELABORATE
AND NOT AT ALL CAVE-LIKE.

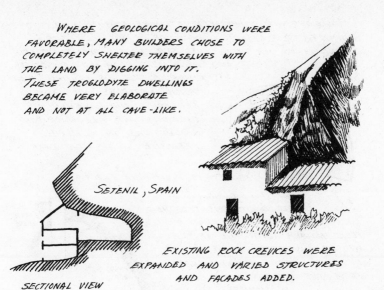

SETENIL, SPAIN

SECTIONAL VIEW

EXISTING ROCK CREVICES WERE
EXPANDED AND VARIED STRUCTURES
AND FACADES ADDED.

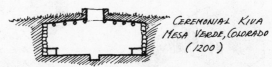

CEREMONIAL KIVA
MESA VERDE, COLORADO
(1200)

KIVAS WERE CIRCULAR STONE STRUCTURES SUNKEN INTO
THE GROUND, WITH A WOOD CEILING THAT SUPPORTED A
LAYER OF EARTH. ORIGINALLY THESE WERE CERE-
MONIAL BUILDINGS, BUT LATER DWELLINGS
TOOK THIS SHAPE ALSO.

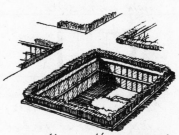

TROGLODYTE DWELLINGS
NORTHERN CHINA
    THESE HOMES, CARVED
INTO SOFT LOESS, LEFT THE
SURFACE FREE FOR FARMING.

UNESCO HEADQUARTERS
PARIS

29

While the first step taken to insure staying warm is to minimize the dwelling's exposure to the cold, the second is to maximize the structure's ability to gain and hold heat from natural sources, primarily the sun. Siting, orientation, materials used, zoning of spaces, and placement of openings are all major considerations in achieving effective solar heat gain.

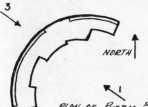

PLAN OF PUEBLO BONITO, NEW MEXICO (A.D. 919)

The Pueblo Indians at Pueblo Bonito oriented their living complex so that it took maximum advantage of the winter sun from dawn (1) to dusk (2) while providing shade from the hot afternoon sun in summer (3).

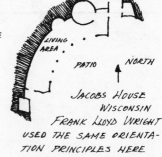

JACOBS HOUSE WISCONSIN FRANK LLOYD WRIGHT USED THE SAME ORIENTATION PRINCIPLES HERE IN 1943.

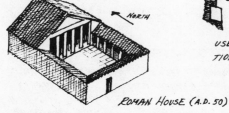

ROMAN HOUSE (A.D. 50)

This plan offered a protected sunny court plus a large southern exposure for the main living space

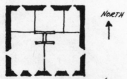

PLAN OF QUEBEC HOUSE (1832)

Note the predominance of windows on the South side for solar heat gain.

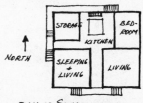

PLAN OF SWISS HOUSE

The zoning of spaces in this house puts the major living areas on the sunny south side while storage and other less used spaces are on the North.

SOUTH DAKOTA FARMHOUSE
EARLY 20th CENTURY

THIS HOUSE IS ORIENTED SO THAT THE MAJOR LIVING SPACE HAS A WARM, PROTECTED SOUTHERN EXPOSURE. THE KITCHEN/WORK EL ON THE LEFT (WEST) SHADES MUCH OF THE SOUTH WALL FROM THE HOT AFTERNOON SUN IN THE SUMMER.

COMPASS TERMITE MOUND
AUSTRALIA

THESE TALL (UP TO 13 FEET) BLADE-LIKE MOUNDS ARE ORIENTED ON A PRECISE NORTH/SOUTH LINE. THE TERMITES SPEND THE MORNINGS ON THE EAST SIDE AND THEN MOVE TO THE WEST (WITH THE SUN) IN THE AFTERNOON.

WALL OF PUBLIC BATHS POMPEII (80 B.C.) THIS SOUTH-FACING GLAZED WALL ADDED A LARGE AMOUNT OF SOLAR HEAT TO THE BATHING SPACES INSIDE.

COLONIAL SALTBOX HOUSE
NEW HAMPSHIRE (1860's)

THE MAJORITY OF FIRST- AND SECOND-FLOOR WINDOWS FACED SOUTH FOR SOLAR HEAT GAIN WHILE MOST OF THE NORTH SIDE WAS ROOF TO OFFER PROTECTION FROM THE NORTH WINDS.

ENTRANCE
(BY LADDER)

3
2
1

SECTION THROUGH ACOMA PUEBLO
NEW MEXICO (A.D. 900)

STORAGE SPACES (1) AND SLEEPING AREAS (2) TAKE UP LOWER AND NORTH-FACING PARTS OF BUILDING WITH THE MAIN LIVING AREA (3) BEING ABOVE AND FACING SOUTH.

THE DESIRE FOR SOLAR HEAT AND NATURAL
LIGHT PUT GREAT EMPHASIS ON THE
DESIGN AND USE
OF WINDOWS.

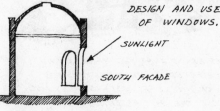

SUNLIGHT

SOUTH FACADE

ROMAN HELIOCAMINVS
OSTIA   (1ST CENTURY)
THE GLAZED SOUTH WALL ADDED
INTENSE HEAT TO THE PUBLIC
BATHS WHILE ALSO KEEPING
IN THE WARM MOIST AIR.

NEW MEXICO (1816)
PIECES OF SELENITE (CRYSTAL-
LIZED GYPSUM) WERE USED
AS A GLAZING.

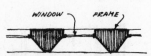

WINDOW   FRAME

PLAN OF STONE WINDOW FRAMES
MEDIEVAL ENGLAND
THE BEVELED SASH ADMITTED
A WIDER ANGLE OF SUNLIGHT
WITHOUT AN INCREASE IN
ACTUAL WINDOW SIZE.

GUARDA, PORTUGAL
THIS STRUCTURE'S BEVELED
SASH AND SILLS SERVE THE
SAME PURPOSE.

EARLY GREECE
PROJECTING SOLARIA ADDED
HEAT AND LIGHT TO HOMES.

TUCSON, ARIZONA
THIS CONTEMPORARY HOUSE USES
A SUNSPACE FOR DIRECT SOLAR GAIN.

THERMAL MASS

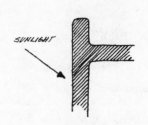

SUNLIGHT

IN HOT, ARID AREAS, DENSE HEAT-ABSORBING MATERIALS CAN MODERATE THE LARGE DAILY TEMPERATURE FLUCTUATIONS BY ABSORBING HEAT DURING THE DAY AND SLOWLY RELEASING IT AT NIGHT.

THERMAL MASS
AS A MODERATOR OF TEMPERATURE SWINGS

OUTSIDE TEMP. ———
INSIDE TEMP. – – –

A   B   C

TIME OF DAY: 6 A.M.   NOON   6 P.M.   12 P.M.   6 A.M.

THE DEGREE OF TEMPERATURE VARIATION OUTSIDE (A) IS GREATLY REDUCED INSIDE (B) BECAUSE THE PEAK EFFECT OF THE DAY'S HEAT IS DELAYED BY THE THERMAL MASS TO A TIME WHEN IT IS COUNTERBALANCED BY THE COOL OF THE NIGHT. THUS THE BUILDING HELPS COOL ITSELF DURING THE DAY AND HEAT ITSELF AT NIGHT. THIS TIME DELAY IN THERMAL EFFECTS IS CALLED THE THERMAL LAG.

MATERIALS TRADITIONALLY USED IN THIS WAY INCLUDE MUD, ADOBE, STONE, BRICK, TILE, AND CONCRETE.

MUD AND STONE
MATAKAN HOUSE
NORTHERN CAMAROON

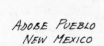

ADOBE PUEBLO
NEW MEXICO

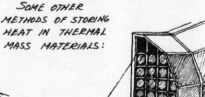

SOME OTHER
METHODS OF STORING
HEAT IN THERMAL
MASS MATERIALS:

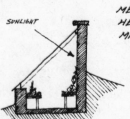

SUNLIGHT

BRICK THERMAL WALL
GREENHOUSE (1700'S)

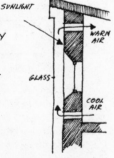

"DRUMWALL"
ALBUQUERQUE, NEW MEXICO
(WATER-FILLED DRUMS BEHIND GLASS) (1975)

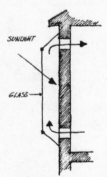

SUNLIGHT

GLASS →

A THICK
MASONRY WALL DIRECTLY
BEHIND SOUTH-FACING
GLASS CAN STORE A
GREAT DEAL OF HEAT,
AND AIR CAN FLOW
BETWEEN THE WALL
AND GLASS TO HELP
DISTRIBUTE THAT HEAT.

MORSE WALL (1881)

SUNLIGHT

WARM
AIR

GLASS →

COOL
AIR

TROMBE WALL
(OR TROMWALL) (1981)

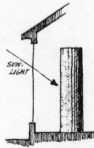

SUN-
LIGHT

WATER CAN STORE MORE
HEAT THAN OTHER
MATERIALS, BUT
SPECIAL CHEMI-
CALS DESIGNED TO
CHANGE PHASE (FROM
SOLID TO LIQUID) AT
CERTAIN TEMPERA-
TURES CAN DO
EVEN BETTER.

WATER COLUMNS
CONCORD, NEW HAMPSHIRE
(1980)

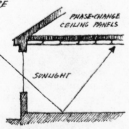

PHASE-CHANGE
CEILING PANELS

SUNLIGHT

PHASE-CHANGE CEILING
PANELS IN EXPERIMENTAL
HOUSE, MASSACHUSETTS (1975)

NATURAL INSULATION

MANY EARLY
DWELLINGS WERE
PROTECTED BY A
BLANKET OF EARTH
TO ACT AS AN
INSULATOR.

EARLY ARMENIAN DWELLING
THIS EARTH-SHELTERED STRUCTURE
ACCOMMODATED BOTH HUMANS (ON
THE RIGHT) AND ANIMALS.

MANDAN EARTH LODGE
UPPER MISSOURI VALLEY

INUIT IGLOO, CANADA
BOTH ICE AND SNOW ACT
AS INSULATORS AGAINST THE
SUB-ZERO TEMPERATURES
AND HARSH WINDS.

FARMHOUSE, HOKKAIDO,
JAPAN

THE ROOF IS STRONG AND
STEEPLY PITCHED TO CARRY
THE LOAD OF A DEEP
BLANKET OF SNOW
FOR INSULATION.

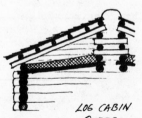

LOG CABIN
QUEBEC
A LAYER OF EARTH ON
THE CEILING ACTS AS INSU-
LATION.

INSULATION

IN COLD WEATHER, ADDITIONAL LAYERS OF HEAVY FELT BLANKETS, OR MUNDAHS, WERE PLACED ON THE YURT FOR EXTRA INSULATION.

KIRGHIZIAN YURT

IN SOME INSTANCES HAY BALES WERE USED AS STRUCTURAL ELEMENTS, AND THEY ALSO PROVIDED GOOD INSULATION.

HAY BALE BARN NEBRASKA (1910)

HAY BALES WERE (AND STILL ARE) USED AS INSULATION AROUND HOUSE FOUNDATIONS IN NEW ENGLAND. IN THE MIDWEST, MANURE IS SOMETIMES USED FOR THIS PURPOSE.

NEW HAMPSHIRE HOUSE (1850)

WASPS MAKE PAPER WITH WHICH THEY BUILD THEIR NESTS. THE THIN SHELL WITH MANY AIR POCKETS INSULATES AS WELL AS 16 INCHES OF BRICK.

WALL OF PAPER WASP NEST

EARLY HOME BUILDERS FILLED THE CAVITY BETWEEN INNER AND OUTER WALLS WITH PAPER OR STRAW FOR INSULATION. BUILDERS TODAY USE FIBERGLASS, CELLULOSE, FOAMS, AND OTHER MATERIALS.

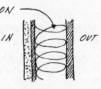

INSULATION

IN   OUT

STOPPING HEAT LOSS CAUSED BY THE INFILTRATION OF COLD AIR

CHINKING OF MUD PLUS SKINS HUNG ON THE INSIDE WALL STOPPED UP THE AIR LEAKS BETWEEN LOGS.

LOG CABIN WALL U.S. (1800's)

PLASTER ON STONE WALLS SEALED GAPS.

PENNSYLVANIA HOUSE (1800)

SIMPLE EXTERIOR SOLID SHUTTERS

NEW YORK (1706)

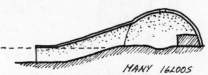

BRIEFLY HEATING AN IGLOO AFTER CONSTRUCTION FORMS AN ICE LAYER INSIDE THAT SEALS CRACKS. SKINS HUNG INSIDE HELP INSULATE, TOO.

INUIT IGLOO, CANADA

MANY IGLOOS HAVE THE ENTRANCE BELOW THE LIVING LEVEL SO THAT THE WARM AIR (WHICH RISES) DOES NOT ESCAPE.

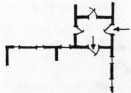

EARLY FARMHOUSES IN THE MIDWEST AND EASTERN U.S. HAD A "DOUBLE ENTRY" - THE ATTACHED SPACE ACTED AS A BUFFER TO PREVENT DIRECT LOSS OF HEAT.

REVOLVING DOORS REDUCE HEAT LOSS BY ELIMINATING PATHS FOR DIRECT AIR FLOW BETWEEN INSIDE AND OUTSIDE.

EXTERIOR PANEL
SHUTTERS, VIRGINIA
(1700's)

FUTURASAN SHRINE, NIKKO, JAPAN
THE EXTERIOR SHUTTERS (A) HERE ARE
SOLID FOR INSULATION WHILE THE
INTERIOR ONES (B) ARE TRANSLUCENT
TO ADMIT NATURAL LIGHT. METAL
BRACKETS FROM THE CEILING HOLD
THEM OPEN.

SLIDING INDIAN SHUTTERS
YORK, MAINE (1800)

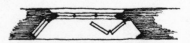

BIFOLD INTERIOR SHUTTERS
PHILADELPHIA (1850)
THESE FOLD BACK NEATLY INTO THE
WALL.

ICEHOUSE WINDOW
SHAKER VILLAGE,
HANCOCK, MASSACHUSETTS
EARLY USE OF MULTIPLE GLAZING
TO CUT DOWN HEAT FLOW

CONTEMPORARY HOUSE
VERMONT
PANELS ARE LOWERED
OVER WINDOWS AT
NIGHT TO REDUCE HEAT
LOSS.

IN REVIEW, TO BEST RETAIN HEAT AND PROTECT AGAINST COLD, BUILDERS MUST:

1) MINIMIZE THE STRUCTURE'S EXPOSURE TO THE COLD;
2) MINIMIZE THE HEAT LOSS FROM THE STRUCTURE BY USING VARIOUS INSULATING TECHNIQUES;
3) MAXIMIZE THE NATURAL HEAT GAINS FROM SUN AND EARTH.

AFTER THESE GUIDELINES HAVE BEEN FOLLOWED THERE MAY STILL BE A NEED FOR ADDITIONAL HEATING. THIS CAN BE SUPPLIED BY A VARIETY OF MEANS.

SOME ANTS HEAT THEIR COLONY BY TAKING TURNS SITTING OUT IN THE SUN SOAKING UP ITS RADIANT HEAT AND THEN GOING BACK INSIDE TO ACT AS LIVING PORTABLE HEATERS. WASPS AND BEES CAN HEAT THEIR HIVES WITH THE INCREASED BODY HEAT GENERATED THROUGH THE MUSCULAR EXERTION OF FLEXING THEIR ABDOMENS OR FLAPPING THEIR WINGS.

THE EARLY HUMAN SHELTERS RELIED PRIMARILY ON TWO HEAT SOURCES:
1) FIRE
2) BODY HEAT FROM PEOPLE AND ANIMALS

EUROPEAN LONGHOUSE (1100)
THE ANIMALS IN THE BYRE HELPED TO HEAT THIS PRIMITIVE SHELTER.

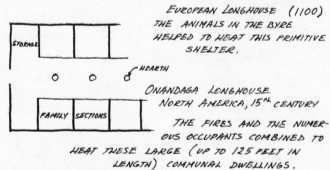

ONANDAGA LONGHOUSE
NORTH AMERICA, 15ᵗʰ CENTURY

THE FIRES AND THE NUMEROUS OCCUPANTS COMBINED TO HEAT THESE LARGE (UP TO 125 FEET IN LENGTH) COMMUNAL DWELLINGS.

HEAT PRODUCTION OF AVERAGE PERSON:
SEATED   - 110 WATTS *
LIGHT WORK   - 170 WATTS
HEAVY WORK   - 440 WATTS

* FOR COMPARISON, A 100-WATT INCANDESCENT LIGHT PRODUCES APPROXIMATELY 96 WATTS OF HEAT.

THE BRUSH TURKEY BUILDS ITS BROODING MOUND BY GATHERING A LARGE PILE OF PLANT MATERIAL, PLACING THE EGGS ON TOP, AND COVERING THEM WITH SAND. THE FERMENTATION OF THE PLANTS GENERATES THE HEAT TO INCUBATE THE EGGS.

COMPOST — EGGS — SAND

BRUSH TURKEY BROODING MOUND

A SINGLE WHALE OIL LAMP IN AN IGLOO CAN MAINTAIN A COMFORTABLE TEMPERATURE.

INUIT IGLOO, CANADA

EARLY INDIAN DWELLINGS IN THE SOUTHWESTERN U.S. RELIED UPON AN OPEN FIREPIT FOR HEAT WITH A SMOKE HOLE IN THE EARTH ROOF.

SMOKE HOLE

INDIAN DWELLING, AMERICAN SOUTHWEST (A.D. 500)

EARLY SETTLERS IN JAMESTOWN BUILT HUTS THAT HAD WALLS OF WATTLE (STICKS WITH INTERWOVEN TWIGS) AND DAUB (MUD), AND ROOFS OF THATCH. THE HOUSES HAD OPEN HEARTHS AND NO CHIMNEYS EXCEPT FOR THE SHORT OUTLET AT THE ROOF.

JAMESTOWN, VIRGINIA (CA. 1608)

THROUGHOUT HISTORY THE MOST COMMON
FUEL USED FOR SPACE HEATING HAS
BEEN WOOD.

JAPANESE RO

HIBACHI

FOR CENTURIES IN JAPAN
WOOD HAS BEEN PROCESSED INTO
CHARCOAL, WHICH IS THEN BURNED
IN HEARTHS SET INTO THE FLOOR (ROS)
OR IN PORTABLE HIBACHIS. CHARCOAL COMBUSTION
YIELDS VERY LITTLE SMOKE, SO
CHIMNEYS WERE NOT BUILT.

DUTCH HEARTH, 17th CENTURY

THE WIDE, DEEP HEARTH WITH ITS
CANTILEVERED HOOD BROUGHT THE
FIRE'S WARMTH RIGHT OUT INTO
THE ROOM.

ENGLISH HEARTH
16th CENTURY
THE BIG HEARTH HAD
SPACE ENOUGH FOR A
NICE WARM WORK SPACE
AND A WINDOW.

QUAKER FIREPLACES
19th CENTURY

THE CORNER
FIREPLACE
RADIATES HEAT
WELL THROUGHOUT THE ROOM, AND
THIS BACK-TO-BACK SCHEME
ALLOWS TWO FIREPLACES TO SHARE
ONE CHIMNEY, THEREBY REDUCING
THE AMOUNT OF CONSTRUCTION
THAT IS REQUIRED.

HOODED FIREPLACE WITH
A BRICK HEARTH
NEW MEXICO (19th CENTURY)

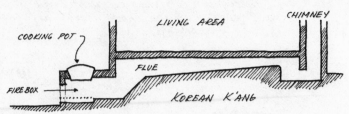

COOKING POT

LIVING AREA

CHIMNEY

FIREBOX

FLUE

KOREAN K'ANG

IN THIS HEATING SYSTEM THE HOT GASES FROM THE FIRE WEAVE UNDER THE DWELLING FLOOR BEFORE GOING OUT THE CHIMNEY. THE ENTIRE FLOOR THEN ACTS AS A RADIANT HEATER. THE ROMANS USED A SIMILAR SYSTEM BUT WERE ABLE TO HEAT ALL SIX SURFACES SURROUNDING THE SPACE.

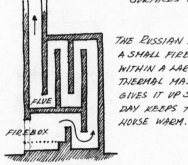

FLUE

FIREBOX

RUSSIAN STOVE

THE RUSSIAN MASONRY STOVE CONSISTS OF A SMALL FIREBOX AND A WINDING FLUE WITHIN A LARGE MASONRY MASS. THIS THERMAL MASS STORES THE HEAT AND GIVES IT UP SLOWLY. ONE SMALL FIRE PER DAY KEEPS THE HOUSE WARM.

THE AUSTRIAN KACHELOFEN USES THERMAL MASS PRINCIPLES LIKE THE RUSSIAN STOVE AND IS USUALLY TILED. THE LOADING DOOR IS OFTEN BEHIND THE WALL IN AN ADJACENT ROOM OR HALLWAY.

KACHELOFEN

IN THIS HOUSE IN BREWSTER, MASSACHUSETTS THE CHIMNEY IS CENTRALLY LOCATED SO IT CAN GIVE ITS HEAT TO THE INTERIOR SPACES RATHER THAN TO THE OUTDOORS.

THE INVENTION OF THE WOODSTOVE ALLOWED THE HEAT SOURCE TO BE MOVED OUT INTO THE ROOM. SUCH A CENTRAL LOCATION GAVE BALANCED RADIATION AND CONVECTION THROUGHOUT WHILE THE LONG RUN OF STOVEPIPE TO THE CHIMNEY SERVED AS AN ADDITIONAL RADIATOR OF HEAT THAT WAS PREVIOUSLY LOST UP THE CHIMNEY.

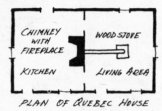

PLAN OF QUEBEC HOUSE

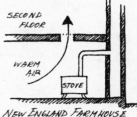

NEW ENGLAND FARMHOUSE

NATURAL CONVECTIVE CURRENTS RATHER THAN FANS WERE THE DRIVING FORCES BEHIND THE DISTRIBUTION OF THE WOODSTOVE'S HEAT. GRATES WERE USUALLY PLACED IN THE CEILING ABOVE THE STOVE TO ALLOW WARM AIR TO RISE TO THE SECOND FLOOR.

POTBELLY STOVE

THE SOMEWHAT SPHERICAL SHAPE OF THE OLD POTBELLY STOVE MADE IT A VERY EFFECTIVE RADIATOR.

IN ORDER TO YIELD AS MUCH HEAT AS POSSIBLE, MANY WOODSTOVE DESIGNS INCORPORATED LARGE HEAT EXCHANGERS TO EXTRACT HEAT FROM THE HOT FLUE PIPES.

VERMONT SOAPSTONE STOVE

BECAUSE OF THEIR GREAT THERMAL MASS, SOAPSTONE STOVES HEAT UP AND COOL DOWN SLOWLY, WHICH RESULTS IN A RELATIVELY EVEN HEAT OVER A LONG PERIOD.

ANOTHER METHOD OF EFFECTIVELY DISTRIBUTING
HEAT IS TO TRANSPORT THE HEAT
SOURCE TO WHERE IT
IS NEEDED.

JAPANESE PORTABLE
KEROSENE HEATER
(USED NOW)

PORTABLE CHARCOAL BRAZIER
USED IN OLYNTHVS, GREECE
(400 B.C.)

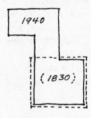

CONTEMPORARY METHODS
OF DISTRIBUTING HEAT
WITH FANS AND PUMPS
HAVE PERMITTED HOUSES
TO BECOME SPREAD OUT
AND FRAGMENTED. THIS
RESULTS IN A SPATIAL
CONFIGURATION THAT IS MUCH
LESS EFFICIENT TO HEAT THAN THE OLD
CENTRALIZED PLAN (SEE HOUSE
PLAN TO THE LEFT).

RADIATORS

BOILER

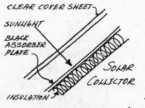

CLEAR COVER SHEET
SUNLIGHT
BLACK
ABSORBER
PLATE
SOLAR
COLLECTOR
INSULATION

ONE OF THE MOST RAPIDLY DEVEL-
OPING HEATING TECHNOLOGIES IS
SOLAR. A BASIC ACTIVE SOLAR
SYSTEM CONSISTS OF A COLLECTOR,
A DISTRIBUTION NETWORK, AND
A HEAT STORAGE RESERVOIR.
THE COLLECTOR ABSORBS THE SUN'S HEAT AND
TRANSFERS IT TO A FLUID (USUALLY AIR
OR WATER). THE HEAT IS THEN
EITHER STORED OR USED IMMEDI-
ATELY TO HEAT THE HOUSE OR
THE DOMESTIC WATER.

MOST CONTEMPORARY SOLAR
HOMES COMBINE ACTIVE SYSTEMS
(THOSE NEEDING ENERGY INPUT)
AND PASSIVE SYSTEMS SUCH AS
ATTACHED GREENHOUSES, EXTRA
SOUTH GLAZING, THERMAL MASS,
AND MANY MORE.

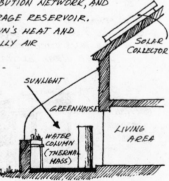

SOLAR
COLLECTOR

SUNLIGHT

GREENHOUSE

WATER
COLUMN
(THERMAL
MASS)

LIVING
AREA

CONTEMPORARY SOLAR HOUSE

BIOCLIMATIC INDEX

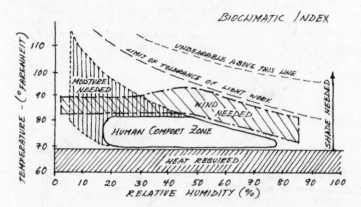

THE ABOVE BIOCLIMATIC INDEX OUTLINES THE RELATION-SHIP BETWEEN TEMPERATURE, HUMIDITY, AND HUMAN COMFORT. WHEN CONDITIONS ARE ABOVE THE HUMAN COMFORT ZONE IT IS NECESSARY TO INTRODUCE A COOLING INFLUENCE SUCH AS SHADING, VENTILATION, OR ADDED MOISTURE.

THIS INFORMATION HAS MANY IMPORTANT HOUSING DESIGN IMPLICATIONS IN AREAS WHERE COOLING IS REQUIRED. THESE GUIDELINES VARY WITH THE CLIMATE:

A) HOT-ARID CLIMATE: 1) TAKE ADVANTAGE OF THE BROAD DAILY TEMPERATURE VARIATION BY USING MATERIALS THAT ABSORB THE DAY'S HEAT FOR RERADIATION AT NIGHT AND BY TRAPPING AND HOLDING COOL NIGHT AIR, 2) GIVE PLENTY OF SHADING, AND 3) MINIMIZE DAYTIME VENTILATION

B) HOT-HUMID CLIMATE: 1) SITE, ORIENT, AND CONSTRUCT THE HOUSE TO TAKE MAXIMUM AD-VANTAGE OF NATURAL VENTILATION, 2) USE POROUS NON-HEAT-ABSORBING MATERIALS, AND 3) SUPPLY ADEQUATE SHADING.

THE WAYS IN WHICH THE HUMAN BODY DISSIPATES HEAT:

RADIATION	-	44 %
CONVECTION	-	32 %
EVAPORATION	-	21 %
CONDUCTION	-	3 %

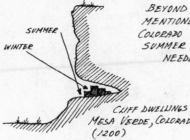

BEYOND THE ADVANTAGES PREVIOUSLY
MENTIONED, THE CLIFFS AT MESA VERDE,
COLORADO OFFERED SHADE FROM THE HOT
SUMMER SUN BUT ADMITTED THE SUN'S
NEEDED WARMTH IN WINTER.

SUMMER
WINTER

CLIFF DWELLINGS
MESA VERDE, COLORADO
(1200)

HERE, THE SHADE OFFERED
BY TREES IS AUGMENTED BY A
SUSPENDED, GRASS-COVERED NET
TO SHIELD THE HAMMOCK.

COLUMBIA

NEW MEXICO

LOCATING DWELLINGS BY RIVERS
OFFERS FRESH WATER AND
TREES FOR SHADE, AND THE
VALLEY TRAPS THE HEAVIER
COOL AIR.

IN AREAS WHERE
WIND IS THE PRIMARY COOLING
AGENT, IT MAY BE ADVANTAGEOUS
TO PUT THE HOUSE ON AN EXPOSED HILL.

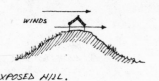

WINDS

IN ADDITION TO SUPPLYING
AN ALL-IMPORTANT
SANCTUARY FROM
CLOUDS OF MOSQUITOES,
THESE HOUSES, PLACED IN
TREES OUT IN THE
WATER, WERE COOL
RETREATS FROM THE
TROPICAL HEAT.

ORINOCO DELTA, VENEZUELA (1600)

SHADING

EARLY MAN, LIKE THE APES, RELIED CHIEFLY UPON THE PLANTS AROUND HIM TO CREATE SHADE.

IN THIS CASE, A LEAN-TO OF BRANCHES AND LEAVES PROTECTS THE HAMMOCK OCCUPANT FROM RAIN AND SUN.

PRIMITIVE LEAN-TO

THE NAVAHO SUMMER SHELTER, OR RAMADA, HAS A SIMPLE POLE FRAME AND A ROOF OF POLES AND BRUSH. IT GIVES SHADE WHILE LETTING THE COOL BREEZES FLOW THROUGH.

THE YOKUT INDIANS OF SOUTHERN CALIFORNIA BUILT POLE AND BRUSH SHADE ROOFS OVER WHOLE GROUPS OF HUTS.

YOKUT TULE LODGE, CALIFORNIA

SENUFO OUTDOOR KITCHEN, IVORY COAST

IN MANY WARM CLIMATES SHELTER TAKES THE FORM OF AN UMBRELLA TO PROTECT FROM THE RAIN AND TO GIVE SHADE FROM THE SUN.

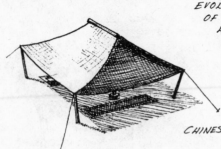

IN ASIA THE TENT HAS EVOLVED OVER THOUSANDS OF YEARS INTO A VERY HIGHLY DEVELOPED AND SOMETIMES ELABORATE SHELTER FROM SUN AND RAIN.

CHINESE MILITARY PAVILION

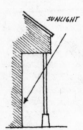

SUNLIGHT

SOME BUILDINGS HAVE PROJECTING UPPER STORIES THAT, IN ADDITION TO ADDING MORE SPACE, CREATE A COVERED WALK BELOW AND SHADE MUCH OF THE LOWER RECESSED WALL.

SECTION OF CASA ISOLANI

CASA ISOLANI, BOLOGNA, ITALY (1200)

ANOTHER WAY TO KEEP THE SUN FROM OVERHEATING A BUILDING IS TO CREATE A HIGHLY TEXTURED FACADE SO THAT THE PROTRUSIONS ACTUALLY SHADE THE REST OF THE WALL.

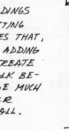

MOUSGOUM HOMESTEAD NORTHERN CAMEROON

DOGON HOUSE SANGA, MALI

Using Vegetation for Seasonal Shade

TRELLIS, OR PERGOLA, OVER DOORWAY

TRANI HOUSE
APULIA, ITALY

WIRE LATTICE USED AS A TRELLIS FOR VINES SHADING COURT

SHADED COURT, GRANADA, SPAIN

NORTH

HOUSE

TREES

AN OLD NEW ENGLAND TRADITION IS TO PLANT HUSBAND AND WIFE TREES TO GIVE SUMMER SHADE TO THE HOUSE'S SOUTH SIDE WHEN IT IS MOST VULNERABLE IN THE MORNING AND EVENING.

FARMHOUSE
NEW HAMPSHIRE

IN MANY AREAS ELABORATE IRON GRILLWORK IS USED AS A LATTICE FOR VINES TO SHADE THE HOUSE.

DOUBLE-TRELLISED HOUSE IN NEW ORLEANS, LOUISIANA

IN MOST WARM CLIMATES
A GREAT DEAL OF THE ACTIVITY
TAKES PLACE OUTSIDE. THE
NEED TO SUPPLY SHADE IN
OUTDOOR PUBLIC PLACES
SPAWNED A WIDE VARIETY
OF SHADES AND
SUNSCREENS.

CANVAS AWNINGS, OR TOLDOS, UNFURLED
BETWEEN BUILDINGS   SEVILLE, SPAIN

RIGID FRAMES
ROOFED WITH SPACED
POLES ALSO SHADE
STREETS AND WALK-
WAYS EFFECTIVELY.

COVERED STREET
TAOS, NEW MEXICO

SIMPLE POLE-SUPPORTED
AWNING

MYKONOS, GREECE

WOOD LATTICE SUNSCREEN

AFRICAN BAZAAR

50

COVERED PORCHES
HAVE BEEN USED
FOR THOUSANDS OF
YEARS AS A SHADY
SANCTUARY FROM
THE HOT SUN.

DOUBLE HOUSE
SAN ANTONIO, TEXAS

ARCADES CAN PROVIDE
BOTH SHADE AND
PROTECTION FROM
RAIN AND SNOW.

DORDOGNE, FRANCE

PORCH ROOFS SUPPLY
SHADE AND CAN ALSO BE
USED AS ADDITIONAL
LIVING OR SLEEPING
AREAS.

SANTA FE,
NEW MEXICO

SOME HOUSES HAVE
PORCHES THAT
WRAP ALMOST
ENTIRELY AROUND
THEM.

HACIENDA, VENEZUELA

THE RAISED BALCONY, OR LOGGIA, IS A VERY COMMON SIGHT IN WARM CLIMATES. THESE STRUCTURES CREATE RELATIVELY PRIVATE LIVING SPACES THAT ARE EXPOSED TO THE COOLING BREEZES. THEY ALSO CAN SHADE THE LOWER FLOOR.

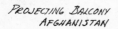

LOGGIA, PEDRAZA, SPAIN

PROJECTING BALCONY
AFGHANISTAN

THIS LOGGIA IS PARTLY WINDOWED, PARTLY OPEN, AND PARTLY FITTED WITH LOUVERED SHUTTERS.

MYKONOS, GREECE

THIS LOGGIA FACES A SERENE, SHADED COURT AND ALSO SHELTERS THE PORCH BELOW, WHICH ACTS AS THE ENTRANCE.

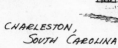

CHARLESTON,
SOUTH CAROLINA

Shading the Openings

In a warm climate it is important to design openings that admit the cooling winds but not the heat of the sun. One way to do this is to recess the window or door so that the depth of the wall shades much of the opening.

Pueblo window
New Mexico

Doorway, Afghanistan

Shading devices such as roofs, shutters, awnings, lattices, and louvers are also effective.

Afghan window
Maydan Valley

Horizontally hinged shutters double as shades.
Kavalla, Greece

This window combines shutters, lattice screens, and louvers for good ventilation and plenty of privacy.

Jeddah,
Saudi Arabia

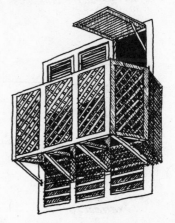

FOR CENTURIES LOUVERED
SHUTTERS HAVE BEEN USED
AS A MEANS OF SHUTTING
OUT THE HOT SUN BUT
ALLOWING THE COOLING
BREEZES TO FLOW
THROUGH.

DOORWAY WITH
LOUVERED SHUTTER, FOSSACESIA, ITALY

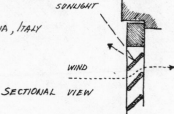

SECTIONAL VIEW

CONTEMPORARY LOUVERED
AWNING SHUTTER, FLORIDA

ADJUSTABLE, VERTICAL-AXIS
LOUVERS, OR VANES, ARE ALSO
VERY EFFECTIVE SHADING
DEVICES.

CONTEMPORARY HOUSE
RIO DE JANEIRO

OTHER SHADES:

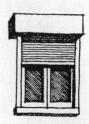

EXTERIOR, METAL
ROLL SHADE
LUXEMBOURG

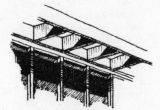

PROJECTING SUNSCREEN
NARA, JAPAN

54

PLACING THE SCREENS
OR LOUVERED SHUTTERS
AWAY FROM THE WINDOWS
CAUSES LESS INTER-
FERENCE WITH THE AIR
FLOW THROUGH
THE HOUSE.

CONTEMPORARY HOUSE
SAN ANTONIO, TEXAS

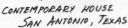

CONTEMPORARY HOUSE
WITH PULLEY-OPERATED
SHUTTER/SHADE
PANELS

SANIBEL ISLAND,
FLORIDA

PROPERLY DESIGNED OVERHANGS
CAN OFFER SHADE FROM
THE HIGH SUMMER SUN (1)
IN TEMPERATE AREAS
AND ADMIT THE
LOW WINTER SUN (2).

SUNLIGHT

THE ROOF OF THIS AFRICAN
HOUSE SHADES THE WINDOW,
AND THE GRASS PATCH
PREVENTS SUNLIGHT
FROM BEING REFLECTED
INSIDE.

CONTEMPORARY OVERHANG
LOS ANGELES, CALIFORNIA

VENTILATION

OPEN AND ELEVATED HOUSES ARE
BUILT IN HOT, HUMID AREAS
PARTLY BECAUSE THEY TAKE
EXCELLENT ADVANTAGE OF
THE COOLING BREEZES.

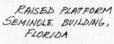

RAISED PLATFORM
SEMINOLE BUILDING,
FLORIDA

TREE HOUSE

NEW GUINEA

THE OPEN PLANNING OF VILLAGES IS ALSO
ESSENTIAL FOR GOOD AIR FLOW.

AIR MOVEMENT THROUGH A
BARI VILLAGE, SUDAN

OPEN SAMOAN HUT

NOTE THE OPEN
SECOND FLOOR IN THIS TWO-
THOUSAND-YEAR-OLD CLAY
MODEL OF A MINOAN
HOUSE.

OPEN PORCH, NEW ORLEANS (1800's)

In the Greek village of Verria homes facing the same street had roofs of different heights for enough separation to ensure good air flow.

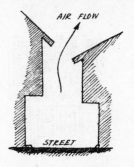

AIR FLOW

VERRIA, EARLY GREECE

STREET

Flat tiles can be arranged in simple patterns to create grilles that admit air but not sunlight.

KSAR-EL-BARKA, MAURITANIA

Lattice walls of reeds and poles are used in many parts of the world to permit ventilation.

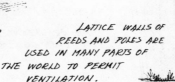

SOUTHERN TANZANIA

The open plan of Japanese houses allows excellent ventilation. Even with the sliding fusumas closed, the louvered transom above lets air flow through.

EXPOSITION HOUSE, MUSEUM OF MODERN ART, NEW YORK (1954)

ONE OF THE MOST WIDELY
EMPLOYED DEVICES THAT GIVES
SHADE AND ALSO ALLOWS
VENTILATION IS THE
LOUVERED
SHUTTER.

MULTIPLE SHUTTER,
MACAO

PORTISOL SHUTTER
DUBROVNIK, YUGOSLAVIA

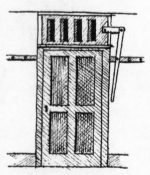

LEVER-OPERATED LOUVER PANEL
TO OPEN OR CLOSE TRANSOM VENT

SHAKER DOOR
HANCOCK, MASSACHUSETTS
(1830)

IN ADDITION TO BEING
SHADED BY THE LOGGIA ROOF,
THIS DOORWAY HAS LOUVERED
SHUTTERS AND A GLASS
TRANSOM VENT FOR
GOOD AIR FLOW.

FAVRIE HOUSE,
NEW ORLEANS (EARLY 1800's)

THE *HIGHLY DECORATIVE*
OPENINGS IN THIS SMITHY
INSURE GOOD
THROUGH-VENTILATION.

BIDA,
CENTRAL NIGERIA

NUMAZU, JAPAN

TRADITIONAL
JAPANESE HOUSES
ARE EQUIPPED WITH
BAMBOO CURTAINS THAT
SCREEN THE SUNLIGHT BUT
LET AIR PASS THROUGH.

STONE VENTILATION GRILLE
GUANAJUATO, MEXICO

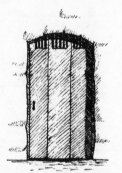

DOOR WITH GRILLE FOR
LIGHT AND AIR
VERACRUZ, MEXICO

THIS DOOR HAS TWO
SMALL, GLAZED SASHES THAT
CAN SLIDE DOWN TO MAKE
OPENINGS FOR VENTILATION.

SHAKER DOOR
CANTERBURY, NEW HAMPSHIRE (1831)

Induced Ventilation

The natural tendency of warmer air to rise can be used as the driving force to ventilate buildings. The venting of warm air at the top will draw cooler air in at the bottom.

Cupola on a New Hampshire barn

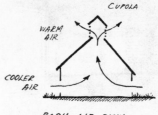

Barn air flow

American top hat barn

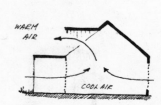

Section through ceremonial underground kiva

Mesa Verde, Colorado

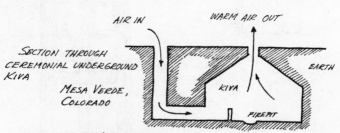

Warm air rising out draws outside air through an underground channel where it is cooled before it enters the kiva.

For millions of years, termite colonies have used thermal currents, or thermosiphoning, to drive their cooling and air purification systems.

Air heated by the colony rises to the top (1) and then flows into the transpiration tubes (2), which act like cooling fins. As the air is cooled, it sinks to the bottom of the colony (3), and the cycle continues. Fresh air is also absorbed through the thin walls of the tubes.

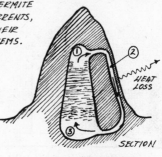

SECTION

TERMITE MOUND

PLAN

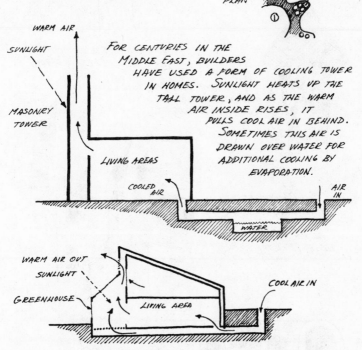

WARM AIR

SUNLIGHT

MASONRY TOWER

LIVING AREAS

COOLED AIR

AIR IN

WATER

For centuries in the Middle East, builders have used a form of cooling tower in homes. Sunlight heats up the tall tower, and as the warm air inside rises, it pulls cool air in behind. Sometimes this air is drawn over water for additional cooling by evaporation.

WARM AIR OUT

SUNLIGHT

GREENHOUSE

LIVING AREA

COOL AIR IN

In this contemporary solar house, the heat generated by sunlight in the greenhouse causes the air to rise and escape, and as it does it pulls cool air into the living areas.

CHANNELING THE WIND

DEVICES THAT COOL
HOUSES BY DIRECTING THE
WIND INSIDE HAVE BEEN
USED FOR CENTURIES.

EGYPTIAN HOUSE WITH WIND SCOOPS
MIDDLE KINGDOM

PERUVIAN WIND SCOOP
(PRE - A.D. 700)

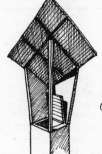

WIND SCOOP WITH TRAP DOOR
WEST PAKISTAN
(USED SINCE 1500's)

ROOFSCAPE
WITH WIND SCOOPS

SIND DISTRICT,
WEST PAKISTAN

WIND SCOOPS
ON ROOFTOPS

HERAT, AFGHANISTAN

THERMAL MASS

As the graph on page 33 shows, the proper use of heat-absorbing, or thermal mass, materials in hot, arid climates can heat a house during the night and cool it during the day. The earth is such a large mass that its temperature stays relatively constant year-round and can help warm a house in the winter and cool it in the summer.

PARTIAL PLAN OF ROMAN SUMMER CAVE

Other solid materials provide thermal mass:

BADAKSHAN DOMED, MUD HOUSE, AFGHANISTAN

MUD AND STONE WALLS

MATAKAM HOUSE CAMEROON

MUD AND STONE DOGON CLIFF DWELLINGS, MALI

STONE CLIFF DWELLINGS MESA VERDE, COLORADO

(1200)

63

THIS HOUSE CONSISTS OF
FIVE HUTS WITH THICK
ADOBE WALLS GROUPED
TO FORM A CENTRAL
COURT, WHICH IS
SHADED BY A
TRELLIS.

MESAKIN QUISAR CLUSTER DWELLING
SUDAN

THE GROUPING OF MANY DWELLINGS IN
A SINGLE, SOLID STRUCTURE PROVIDES A
LARGE THERMAL MASS AND ALSO
LEAVES A MINIMUM OF
SURFACE EXPOSED TO
THE HEAT.

DAMMUSO HOUSE
PANTELLERIA, ITALY

ADOBE PUEBLO
TAOS, NEW MEXICO

VAULTED HOUSES
GREECE

ROOF POND COOLING

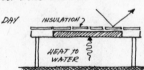

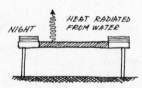

THIS CONTEMPORARY COOLING SYSTEM USES A POND OF WATER
AS A HEAT SINK ON THE ROOF. INSULATED FROM THE SUN
DURING THE DAY, THE POND ABSORBS HEAT FROM THE HOUSE.
UNCOVERED AT NIGHT, IT CAN LOSE ITS HEAT TO THE SKY.

USING COURTYARDS
TO TRAP COOL AIR

THE TENDENCY OF COOLER AIR TO SINK PERMITS AN ENCLOSED COURT TO EFFECTIVELY TRAP THE COOL NIGHT AIR IN HOT, ARID AREAS.

COURT OF SUBTERRANEAN DWELLING, TUNISIA

ASHANTI HOUSE, GHANA

THIS AFRICAN HOUSE HAS AN ENCLOSED COURTYARD, OR "GYAASE," TO GIVE SHADE AND PRIVACY AND TO HOLD COOL AIR.

IN MANY AREAS, A NUMBER OF DWELLINGS ARE BUILT AROUND A CENTRAL COURT, WHICH BECOMES A SANCTUARY FROM THE HEAT.

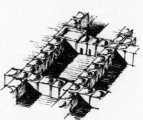

EL OUED, ALGERIA

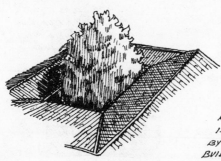

TREE IN ENCLOSED COURTYARD VENEZUELA

THE COURTYARD IS KEPT MUCH COOLER IF IT IS FULLY SHADED BY EITHER THE SURROUNDING BUILDINGS (SEE ABOVE), BY VINES (SEE PAGE 49), OR BY TREES.

WATER WILL EVAPORATE AS IT ABSORBS HEAT FROM THE SURROUNDING AIR. THIS PROCESS, WHICH RESULTS IN THE AIR BEING COOLED, CAN BE USED TO HELP COOL HOUSES IN ARID CLIMATES.

A WATER-SOAKED CLOTH IN THE WINDOW COOLS THE INCOMING AIR.
INDIA

DINING PAVILIONS BUILT OVER WATER
CHINA

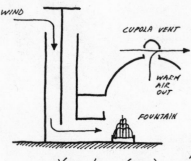

YAZD, IRAN (1400)

IN IRAN SOME BUILDINGS HAVE TOWERS TO CATCH THE WIND AND DIRECT IT INSIDE, WHERE IT IS COOLED AS IT PASSES BY A FOUNTAIN OR POOL. THE WIND ALSO HELPS TO DRAW THE WARM AIR OUT AT THE CUPOLA (SEE PAGE 60).

A FOUNTAIN OR POOL IN A COURTYARD WILL HELP COOL THE AIR, AND THE ENCLOSURE WILL PREVENT THE LOSS OF THAT COOL AIR.

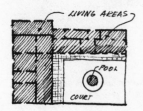

PLAN OF HOUSE WITH COURT AND POOL, VENEZUELA

REMOVING HEAT SOURCES

ONE VERY SIMPLE WAY TO COOL A HOME IS NOT TO HEAT IT. THIS MEANS TRYING TO REMOVE THE THERMAL IMPACT OF SUCH PRIMARY FUNCTIONS AS COOKING AND BATHING.

FOR CENTURIES ONE APPROACH HAS BEEN TO REMOVE THE COOKING WORK FROM THE HOUSE AND TO CREATE A SEPARATE SUMMER KITCHEN.

SUMMER KITCHEN, CURTENI, RUMANIA

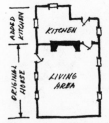

PLAN OF A FARMHOUSE IN PENNSYLVANIA (1709)

HERE, THE KITCHEN IS ATTACHED BUT NOT WITHIN THE LIVING AREA OF THE HOUSE.

PARISH MANSION, VIRGINIA

CHIMNEYS ARE MAJOR HEAT SOURCES. SEPARATING THEM FROM THE HOUSE LESSENS THEIR EFFECT AND ALSO REDUCES THE FIRE HAZARD.

TO HELP COOL HOMES TODAY, THE HEAT PRODUCED BY APPLIANCES SUCH AS STOVES, REFRIGERATORS, CLOTHES DRYERS, AND WATER HEATERS SHOULD BE KEPT AWAY FROM THE LIVING AREAS.

Staying Healthy

People have always had to defend themselves against the environment. Their shelters quickly became their primary defense. It gave refuge from pests, predators, and humans.

This tree dwelling provides an escape from the leeches on the wet ground.

Sakai tree house, Malaya

Grouping dwellings in protective circles is another way of gaining security and privacy.

Plan of Garuns) Compound Upper Volta

This Japanese portable frame with mosquito netting protects infants very effectively.

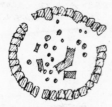

In the Alps, most of the food storage buildings are raised on piers incorporating flat rocks as rodent guards.

Some species of ant have special doorkeepers with enlarged heads. They plug the entrances and admit only the residents, who know the proper antenna tap code.

THE EAGLE USES ITS
AERIE AS A SECURE REFUGE
FROM PREDATORS AND AS AN
OBSERVATION POST FROM
WHICH TO KEEP A SHARP
EYE ON ITS DOMAIN.

LIKE THE EAGLE,
MAN OFTEN BUILT
REFUGES IN HIGH,
STRATEGIC
POSITIONS.

EAGLE'S AERIE

THE ANASAZI INDIANS
OF THE AMERICAN SOUTHWEST
USED LOFTY CRAGS IN SHEER
CLIFFS AS DEFENSIVE POSI-
TIONS AND LOOKOUTS, WHILE
THE RIVER PLAIN WAS LEFT
OPEN FOR AGRICULTURE.

THE WHITE HOUSE
CANYON DE CHELLY
ARIZONA

WHEN LACKING A
LOFTY SITE FOR A
BASTION, THE NEXT BEST
THING WAS TO CREATE A
HILL, USUALLY WITH
TIERED, FORMIDABLE
WALLS.

KUMAMOTO CASTLE, JAPAN

Village in the Caucasus
U.S.S.R.

In medieval Europe there was a pronounced need for fortifications. In some villages, defensive towers became a dominant architectural feature.

A maze of narrow, winding streets would make anyone attacking very vulnerable as they moved through the city.

San Gimignano, Italy

Mont-Saint Michel
France

Limited access and narrow, winding streets gave Mt.-St. Michel a strong defense.

Harman, Rumania

Some entire villages became walled fortresses.

THE USE OF MORE
DURABLE MATERIALS IS A
VERY IMPORTANT PART OF A STRONG
DEFENSE. IN THIS CASTLE WALL,
FOR INSTANCE, THE RESISTANCE
TO FIRE IS INCREASED WITH THE
USE OF TILE, PLASTER, AND
STONE.

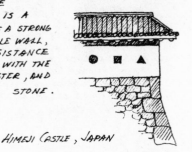

HIMEJI CASTLE, JAPAN

IN THE SAME CASTLE,
SOME OF THE DOORWAYS ARE
METAL-CLAD AND THUS
IMPREGNABLE.

IN 1702 THE TINDER-LIKE
THATCH AND BOARD HOUSES IN THE
SPANISH SETTLEMENT OF ST. AUGUSTINE
WERE BURNED TO THE GROUND BY
CAROLINA COLONISTS. IN REBUILDING
THE TOWN, TABBY, A MIXTURE OF
LIME MORTAR AND
SHELLS, WAS USED
TO MAKE THE
BUILDINGS MORE
RESISTANT
TO FIRE.

THATCH AND BOARD
HOUSE, ST. AUGUSTINE,
FLORIDA (1700)

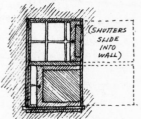

TABBY AND SHINGLE HOUSE
ST. AUGUSTINE,
FLORIDA (1710)

PROTECTING THE WINDOWS:

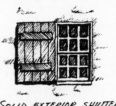

SOLID EXTERIOR SHUTTER
PENNSYLVANIA

(SHUTTERS
SLIDE
INTO
WALL)

SLIDING INDIAN SHUTTERS
NEW HAMPSHIRE

PROTECTING AGAINST INTRUDERS

THIS INGENIOUS FLOOR HAS SPECIAL CLAMPS IN WHICH THE FLOORING NAILS CAN SLIDE, PRODUCING A CHIRPING SOUND. ANYONE WALKING ON THE FLOOR WOULD CAUSE THE CHIRPING AND THUS NO ONE COULD SNEAK UP ON THE EMPORER.

NIGHTINGALE FLOOR
NIJO CASTLE, JAPAN

ONE OF THE BEST SECURITY MEASURES IS TO DESIGN THE ENTRANCE TO A DWELLING SO THAT ANYONE COMING IN IS PRACTICALLY DEFENSELESS.

MANY AFRICAN DWELLINGS' DOORWAYS HAVE HIGH THRESHOLDS AND LOW LINTELS, WHICH FORCE PEOPLE TO BOW AS THEY ENTER. THIS PUTS THEM IN A VULNERABLE POSITION.

ANOTHER EFFECTIVE WAY TO LIMIT ACCESS IS TO REMOVE THE MEANS. THIS DRAWBRIDGE CAN BE WITHDRAWN INTO THE CASTLE.

ROTHESAY CASTLE
SCOTLAND (1312)

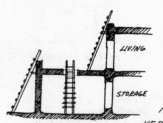

EARLY PUEBLO DWELLINGS HAD LADDERS THROUGH THE ROOF FOR ACCESS. THE LADDER COULD BE DRAWN UP FOR SECURITY. ENTERING BY DESCENDING A LADDER ALSO MADE AN INTRUDER VERY VULNERABLE.

SECTION THROUGH
ACOMA PUEBLO, NEW MEXICO (A.D. 900)

METAL DOOR AND WINDOW GRILLES CAN BAR ACCESS BUT STILL ADMIT LIGHT AND AIR.

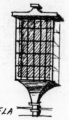

WINDOW GRILLE, VENEZUELA

SLEEPING

DUE TO POOR NIGHT VISION,
PEOPLE ARE VERY VULNERABLE
CREATURES IN THE DARK, SO EARLY
SHELTERS WERE SIMPLY PROTECTED
PLACES IN WHICH TO SLEEP. VERY
SOON, THOUGH, BUILDERS WENT
BEYOND CRUDE SHELTER AND
BEGAN TO PAY ATTENTION TO
COMFORT.

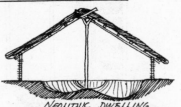

NEOLITHIC DWELLING
KÖLN LINDENTHAL, GERMANY
THE EARTH FLOOR WAS
SCULPTED TO CREATE SEATS,
BEDS, ETC.

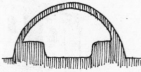

INUIT IGLOO, CANADA

THE AIR AT THE TOP OF A SPACE
IS WARMER (WARM AIR RISES),
SO SLEEPING SHELVES IN
IGLOOS ARE BUILT UP
OFF THE FLOOR.

IN SOME JAPANESE HOMES
A PIT, OR RO, CONTAINING
HOT COALS IS COVERED
BY A WOODEN FRAME
AND IS USED TO PREHEAT
THE BEDDING, OR FUTON.

SOME MASONRY STOVES
HAVE BUILT-IN PLATFORMS THAT
CAN BE USED AS COZY
SLEEPING SHELVES.

TRADITIONAL FINNISH STOVE
WITH GRANDMOTHER SHELF.

IN OTHER AREAS
STAYING COOL IS A PRIMARY
GOAL, AND OFTEN THE ROOF
BECOMES A COOL AND SAFE
SLEEPING LOFT.

GARUNSI HUT, UPPER VOLTA

IN JAPAN THE BEDDING, OR FUTON, IS STORED IN A CLOSET, OR "OSHIIRE," AND BROUGHT OUT AS NEEDED AT NIGHT. THIS SAVES SPACE, BECAUSE DURING THE DAY NO ROOM IS JUST AN UNUSED BEDROOM, AND AT NIGHT ANY ROOM CAN BECOME A BEDROOM.

CLOSET ("OSHIIRE") FOR STORING FUTONS JAPAN

OVER THE CENTURIES PEOPLE HAVE DEVISED MANY INGENIOUS WAYS TO SECRETE BEDS FOR PRIVACY, SECURITY, OR JUST AESTHETICS.

TWO-TIERED BRETON CUPBOARD BED WITH SLIDING DOORS.

PARTITIONED AND CURTAINED BED ALCOVE.

HOLLAND, 17th CENTURY

THE TWO SMALL LEAN-TOS AT EITHER SIDE OF THIS HOUSE WERE ADDED AS EXTRA SLEEPING SPACES.

NANTUCKET WHALER'S HOUSE, 18th CENTURY

EARLY SHELTERS WERE SIMPLY FOR SLEEPING, BUT IN COOLER CLIMATES THERE WAS A NEED TO BRING THE FIRE INSIDE TO COOK AND ADD WARMTH. THE EARLIEST HEARTHS CONSISTED OF SIMPLE OPEN FIREPITS, FROM WHICH THE FIREPLACE EVOLVED.

EARLY JAPANESE SAND HEARTH WITH KETTLE ARM

NORWEGIAN FIREPLACE WITH ADJUSTABLE KETTLE HOLDER

JAPANESE KETTLE HOLDER (THE WOOD BLOCK ON THE ROPE LOCKS THE HEIGHT ADJUSTMENT)

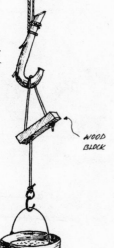

WOOD BLOCK

JAPANESE CHARCOAL FIREPLACE

AS THE FIREPLACE BECAME INTEGRATED INTO THE STRUCTURE OF THE HOUSE A HOOD WAS BUILT TO CAPTURE THE SMOKE, AND THE FIREPLACE GREW INTO A DOMINANT CENTRAL ELEMENT.

PLAN OF AN ENGLISH FIREPLACE (1500's)

THE HOOD OVER THIS FIRE-PLACE COVERS BOTH THE FIRE AND AN INGLENOOK, WHICH HAS A SMALL WINDOW. ONE SIDE OF THE HOOD IS SUPPORTED BY A SHORT WALL CALLED A HECK, WHICH ALSO BUFFERS THE ENTRY.

THIS CORNER FIREPLACE HAS A HOOD OF WATTLE AND DAUB (SEE PAGE 121) SUPPORTED BY A LINTEL THAT WAS MADE FROM THE CROOK OF A TREE.

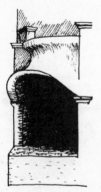

DOUBLE-ARCHED, MASSIVE CORNER FIREPLACE TAOS, NEW MEXICO (1834)

ARCHED HOOD LIVING ROOM FIREPLACE, COPENHAGEN

GRADUALLY THE OPEN FIREPLACE
EVOLVED INTO AN ENCLOSED
FIREBOX THAT WAS MUCH
MORE EFFICIENT AT TRANS-
FERRING HEAT TO THE
COOKING VESSELS.

THE SPANISH
MASONRY STOVE, OR FOGÓN,
HAS SEVERAL SMALL FIRE-
BOXES UNDER A TILE
COOKING SURFACE.

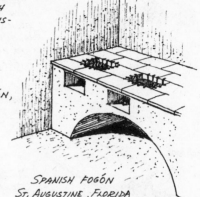

SPANISH FOGÓN
ST. AUGUSTINE, FLORIDA
(1787)

A HOOD TO CARRY OFF THE SMOKE
WAS A WELCOME ADDITION.

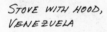

STOVE WITH HOOD,
VENEZUELA

EARLY JAPANESE STOVES
HAD COOKING RECESSES AND A
RICE STEAMER.

JAPANESE STOVE

THE AUSTRIAN KACHELOFEN
DOUBLES AS A COOKSTOVE
AND THE MAIN SOURCE
OF HEAT. ITS TILES
HOLD HEAT FOR
LONG PERIODS.

AUSTRIAN KACHELOFEN

INDIAN OVEN,
OKLAHOMA

THE HEMISPHERICAL OVEN
EXPOSES A MINIMUM OF SURFACE
AREA FOR HEAT LOSS (SEE PAGE 27),
AND IT ALSO GIVES A VERY EVEN
RADIANT HEAT WITHIN. THESE
REASONS, PLUS THE FACT THAT IT IS
EASY TO BUILD, HAVE MADE IT THE
FAVORED FORM FOR CENTURIES.

DOGON OVEN
UPPER VOLTA

STONE

ADOBE

A SMALL FIRE INSIDE HEATS THE
STONE SLAB FOR COOKING
PIKI WAFERS.

PUEBLO INDIAN PIKI OVEN
NEW MEXICO

THE SHAKERS BUILT
LARGE OVENS WITH SEVERAL
REVOLVING RACKS FOR HIGH-VOLUME
BAKING.

SHAKER OVEN
CANTERBURY, NEW HAMPSHIRE
(1876)

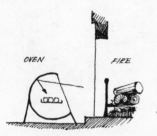

OVEN   FIRE

A SHEET METAL REFLECTOR OVEN
FOCUSES A FIRE'S HEAT ONTO
THE RACK AT ITS
CENTER.

REFLECTOR OVEN
MASSACHUSETTS, 18th CENTURY

JAPANESE TEAPOT
THIS TEAPOT HAS AN EFFICIENT AND
PRACTICAL SHAPE: MAXIMUM SURFACE AREA EXPOSED
TO THE STOVE'S HEAT AND THE MINIMUM AREA EXPOSED
TO THE AIR (DUE TO THE HEMISPHERICAL SHAPE)

THE USE OF TABLES, CHAIRS, AND
UTENSILS FOR DINING HAS
OCCURRED ONLY IN THE
LAST SEVERAL CENTU-
RIES AND, IN MANY
COUNTRIES, IS EVEN NOW
NOT OBSERVED.

HOUSE OF CARO, POMPEII

THIS HOUSE HAS
A U-SHAPED INCLINED
DAIS THAT WAS USED FOR
DINING. THE FOOD WAS
SERVED FROM THE
CENTER AREA.

SECTION THROUGH DAIS AND
SERVICE AREA

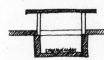

IN SOME OLDER JAPANESE HOMES THERE IS
A RECESS, OR "HORIGOTATSU," IN THE FLOOR
UNDER THE TABLE INTO WHICH HOT COALS
ARE PLACED TO WARM THE FEET
OF THE DINERS.

JAPANESE "HORIGOTATSU"

THE SEATING ARRANGEMENT
IN THE ANCIENT MONESTARY ON
MT. ATHOS ACCOMMODATES LARGE
NUMBERS OF PEOPLE AND
ALLOWS EASY SERVICE ACCESS
AT THE END OF THE
TABLE.

EATING TABLES AT THE MONESTARY
ON MT. ATHOS, GREECE (A.D. 950)

THE FRONT OF THIS
CUPBOARD SWINGS DOWN
TO MAKE A TABLE.

CUPBOARD/TABLE, ALPS

SITTING

Even in Neolithic times, builders were creating raised platforms for sitting, working, and sleeping.

At Çatal Hüyük the plastered dais was covered with mats, cushions, and bedding.

ÇATAL HÜYÜK
ANATOLIA (6000 B.C.)

African villages very often have a shaded resting place where people can quietly gather and chat or just sit.

RESTING PLACE, DAHOMEY

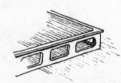

UR PLATFORM, CHINA

This is used as a dais for sitting and reclining.

Raised sections of the floor in many Japanese buildings are used for sitting.

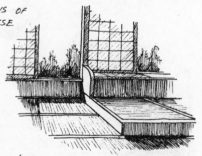

THE THREE-LEGGED STOOL

On very uneven floors it still sits flat.

JAPANESE PAVILION
SHUGAKUIN IMPERIAL VILLA

BATHING

As the house evolved from a crude shelter into a home, bathing received more attention.

This terra-cotta hip bath was found in an elaborately tiled bathroom.

HIP BATH, OLYNTHUS (A.D. 300)

The long drain spout on this triangular terra-cotta sink extended through the wall and emptied into a sewer.

BASIN, OLYNTHUS, GREECE
(A.D. 300)

The use of portable tubs saves the space taken up by a permanent bathroom and allows one to bathe in the warmth of the kitchen.

SHAKER BATHING TUB
SABBATHDAY LAKE, MAINE (1878)

Early Japanese tubs were made of wood with a metal-shielded bottom under which a fire was built.

JAPANESE BATH TUB

Older Japanese homes kept the heat and messy fire of the bath separated from the living areas. The toilet was also separate, but for a different reason.

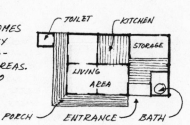

WHEN POSSIBLE, MOST DOMESTIC
ACTIVITIES IN HOT CLIMATES ARE
DONE OUTSIDE, INCLUDING
BATHING.

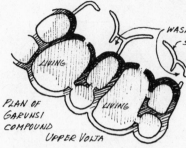

WASHING ENCLOSURES

SHORT WALL

FOR PRIVACY WHILE
WASHING, LOW-WALLED
CUBICLES ARE ATTACHED
TO THESE DWELLING
COMPLEXES BUILT
OF MUD.

PLAN OF
GARUNSI
COMPOUND
UPPER VOLTA

IN JAPAN, BATHING
RECEIVES A GREAT DEAL OF
ATTENTION AND IS PRACTICALLY
AN ART FORM.
AS SHOWN IN THIS CONTEMPORARY
PLAN, THE JAPANESE BELIEVE IN
SEPARATING THE BATH AND
THE TOILET.

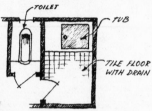

TOILET

TUB

TILE FLOOR
WITH DRAIN

CONTEMPORARY BATH PLAN, JAPAN

ON THE OTHER HAND, THE JAPANESE
HAVE ALSO PRODUCED ONE-PIECE,
PLUG-IN, FIBERGLASS
BATHROOM MODULES.

JAPANESE UNITIZED BATHROOM

SOME EARLY WOOD-FIRED
JAPANESE TUBS WERE INSIDE WHILE
THE FIRE WAS OUTSIDE. THE WATER
CIRCULATED THROUGH PORTS IN THE WALL.

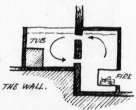

TUB

FIRE

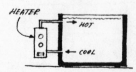

HEATER

HOT

COOL

THE JAPANESE WASH
OUTSIDE OF THE TUB, EITHER BY
LADLING OUT WATER OR USING A
SHOWER NOZZLE, AND THEN THEY GET
IN THE TUB TO SOAK. THE SAME
WATER CAN BE USED SEVERAL
TIMES AND A CIRCULATING
HEATER KEEPS IT VERY HOT.

ELIMINATION

With the establishment of more permanent shelters came the need for a system to deal with sewage. For centuries in China, human waste has been considered a very valuable commodity. It is collected, composted, aged, and then used as a high-quality fertilizer, called night soil.

One of the more primitive waste disposal systems is the outhouse.

The outhouse is simply a sewer pit topped by an enclosed toilet seat. Periodically lime is added to the pit to reduce odors and when it is full it is covered with earth, a new pit is dug, and the outhouse is placed over it.

New York (ca. 1910)

SEAT

PIT

Where to situate the outhouse:
1) put it downwind from the house,
2) keep it away from any water sources,
3) place the woodpile between it and the house so that commuters can bring in some wood on their return trip.

WELL

HOUSE

WOODPILE

OUTHOUSE

PREVAILING WIND

Indoor facilities:

TOILET

MARMOT SUMMER BURROW

When the marmot excavates its burrow it digs a short, spur tunnel that is used as a toilet.

In 3000 B.C. the residents of Olynthus had an underground, brick-lined sewer system that even had lines serving each sentry's post on the city wall.

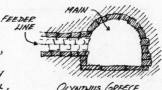

FEEDER LINE

MAIN

OLYNTHUS, GREECE

IN COLD CLIMATES, A TREK TO THE
OUTHOUSE IS NOT TOO POPULAR, SO OFTEN
A PRIVY IS BUILT INTO A CORNER
OF THE BARN.

"DAS STILLE ÖRTCHEN"
(LIT. "THE SMALLEST ROOM")
MATTEN, SWITZERLAND
(17ᵗʰ CENTURY)

TOILET MADE FROM
AN OLD BUTTER
CHURN

SWITZERLAND
(1693)

THE TOILET WAS
FIRST BROUGHT INTO THE
HOUSE AS SIMPLY A BUCKET
WITH A SEAT. THE BUCKET
WAS EMPTIED DAILY AT THE
DUNG HEAP.

PERSONAL HYGIENE HAS ALWAYS
BEEN VERY IMPORTANT TO THE
JAPANESE, WHICH IS EVIDENT IN
THE FIXTURES THAT THEY
HAVE DEVELOPED.

MOST OF THE WORLD'S
CULTURES FAVOR THE SQUAT-
TYPE TOILET BECAUSE IT IS
SIMPLE, IT PROMOTES A NATURAL
POSITION, AND IT IS VERY SANITARY.

JAPANESE PRIVY (CA. 1870)

THIS MODERN JAPANESE TOILET HAS
TWO WATER-SAVING FEATURES: 1) WITH ITS
DUAL FLUSH MODE, LITTLE OR MORE WATER
CAN BE USED AS NECESSARY, AND
2) WATER REFILLING THE TANK CAN BE
USED FOR WASHING ONE'S HANDS.

SPOUT

TANK

CONTEMPORARY
JAPANESE TOILET

JAPANESE URINAL, OR "ASAGAOWA"
(LIT. "MORNING FACE"; IT IS
SUPPOSED TO RESEMBLE THE
FLOWER OF THE MORNING GLORY) (CA. 1870)

Working

     AS CIVILIZATION WENT BEYOND THE HUNTING / GATHERING PHASE AND THE COMPLEXITY OF DOMESTIC LIFE INCREASED, IT BECAME IMPORTANT TO HAVE SPACE IN THE SHELTER FOR NECESSARY TASKS AND FOR STORAGE.

MUKTELE HOUSE, CAMEROON

PLAN

     THE CIRCULAR COMPOUND OF HUTS PROJECTS AND DEFINES AN INNER YARD THAT IS USED AS AN OUTDOOR LIVING AREA, A WORK SPACE, AND A SAFE PLACE TO STORE THINGS.

THE FLAT ROOF HAS BEEN USED IN A VARIETY OF CLIMATES FOR CENTURIES AS A PRACTICAL AND SAFE PLACE FOR WORKING, SLEEPING, DRYING PRODUCE, AND KEEPING ANIMALS.

MOUNTAIN SETTLEMENT
ANDALUSIA, SPAIN

ACOMA PUEBLO
NEW MEXICO (CA. A.D. 900)

     IN MANY AREAS, THE SHAPE OF THE HOUSE IS MANIPULATED TO CREATE BOTH OPEN AND SHADED EXTERIOR AREAS.

     UNDER THESE VAULTS ARE SHADED OUTDOOR LIVING AND WORKING AREAS.

OSTUNI, ITALY

EARLY DWELLINGS IN
TEMPERATE CLIMATES
USUALLY HOUSED ALL
ACTIVITIES UNDER ONE
ROOF TO CONSERVE
HEAT.

ENGLISH LONGHOUSE (PRE-1100)

SOME LATER HOMES
SPLIT THE DWELLING AND THE BYRE
AND CREATED A PROTECTED,
PARTIALLY COVERED COURT BETWEEN
THEM THAT SERVED A VARIETY
OF USES.

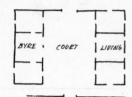

FRENCH FARMHOUSE
PLAN

THE PROJECTING ROOF AND SIDE
WALLS OF THIS BARN CREATE A
PROTECTED OUTSIDE
WORK AREA.

PEASANT DWELLING AND
BARN, FRANCE

NEW ENGLAND BUILDERS CONNECT
THE BARN AND HOUSE WITH A CHAIN OF
WORK SPACES. THIS MINIMIZES THE
NECESSITY OF GOING OUTSIDE IN WINTER.

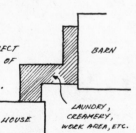

NEW ENGLAND FARMHOUSE
(CA. 1800)

LOGGIAS PROVIDE
LIVING AND WORKING
SPACE THAT IS SHELTERED
FROM BOTH THE RAIN
AND THE SUN.

COURT AND LOGGIA, GREECE

STORAGE

CULTIVATION OF CROPS BEGAN AT LEAST 10,000 YEARS AGO AND WITH THIS SHIFT TO AN AGRARIAN SOCIETY CAME THE NEED TO STORE FOOD. THE GRANARY BECAME THE MOST IMPORTANT BUILDING IN THE SETTLEMENT.

CLAY POT GRANARY, SUDAN

THE GRANARY WAS USUALLY THE FIRST STRUCTURE BUILT IN A SETTLEMENT AND WAS THE MOST METICULOUSLY CRAFTED.

MUD AND THATCH GRANARY, MEXICO

THIS ELABORATELY CARVED STONE GRANARY HAS LARGE FLAT STONES AT THE TOP OF EACH SUPPORTING POST AS A RAT GUARD.

STONE GRANARY GALICIA, SPAIN

LARGE WOODEN GRANARY ELMALI, TURKEY   (19ᵗʰ CENTURY)

THE IMPORTANCE OF RICE TO THE JAPANESE IS CLEARLY EVIDENT FROM A LOOK AT THE TILE AND STUCCO, FIREPROOF STRUCTURE, OR "KURA," WHERE IT IS STORED. THIS FORTRESS-LIKE BUILDING PROTECTS THE RICE FROM BOTH MOISTURE AND FIRE.

"KURA," JAPAN
(CA. 1800)

DETAIL OF THE VAULT-
TYPE DOOR ON A
"KURA."

THIS ELEVATED STRUCTURE, OUT OF THE REACH OF SNOW AND ANIMALS, SERVES AS A STOREHOUSE AND TEMPORARY SHELTER FOR THE LAPPS.

RAISED STOREHOUSE, FINLAND

CORN CRIBS USUALLY HAVE OPEN, SLATTED WALLS TO ALLOW AIR TO FLOW THROUGH AND DRY THE CORN. SOME HAVE ADDITIONAL STORM FLAPS TO KEEP OUT DRIVING RAIN.

IN THIS EXAMPLE NOTE THE RAT GUARDS ON THE POSTS AND THE STEP THAT IS RETRACTED WITH A COUNTERWEIGHT TO PREVENT ANIMALS FROM REACHING THE CORN.

HIGHRISE STOREHOUSE
MEDENINE, TUNISIA

ROOT CELLAR
QUEBEC (1650)

ROOT CELLARS
WERE USUALLY BUILT
ABOVE GROUND TO STAY DRY AND
THEN EARTH WAS PILED OVER
THEM TO MAINTAIN A
CONSTANT, COOL
TEMPERATURE FOR
STORING POTATOES, BEETS,
TURNIPS, ETC.

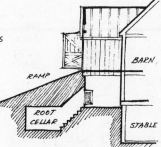

ROOT CELLAR UNDER BARN RAMP
PENNSYLVANIA (1830)

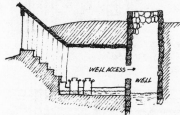

A WET GROUND-CELLAR IS
AN UNDERGROUND STOREROOM
ADJOINING A WELL. POOLS OF
WELL WATER COOLED MILK,
CIDER, ETC.

SPRINGHOUSES KEEP THE
SPRING WATER CLEAN AND SUPPLY
A POOL OF COOL RUNNING WATER
TO CHILL MILK, ETC.

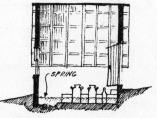

SPRINGHOUSE, PENNSYLVANIA (CA. 1800)

SECTION THROUGH THE STONE WALL OF
A TRULLO DWELLING SHOWING A BUILT-IN
STORAGE NICHE

APULIA, ITALY

A SIMPLE
AND VERSATILE WAY
TO STORE CLOTHES
IS IN A WARDROBE.
THESE MOVABLE
PIECES ARE STILL
VERY POPULAR
IN EUROPE.

THE JAPANESE ARE NOTED FOR
THEIR SIMPLE YET ELEGANT DESIGNS,
SUCH AS THIS UTENSIL HOLDER,
MADE OF NOTCHED
BAMBOO.

THE SHAKERS TRULY
BELIEVE IN "A PLACE FOR EVERY-
THING, AND EVERYTHING IN ITS
PLACE." THIS SERIES OF ATTIC
CLOSETS AND DRAWERS IN CANTER-
BURY, N.H. ATTESTS TO THAT.

ANOTHER FAVORITE STORAGE METHOD
WAS TO HANG THINGS ON PEGS
ON THE WALLS.

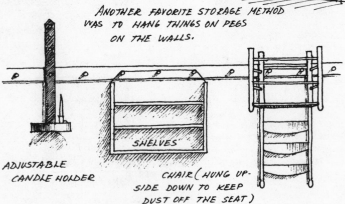

ADJUSTABLE
CANDLE HOLDER

SHELVES

CHAIR (HUNG UP-
SIDE DOWN TO KEEP
DUST OFF THE SEAT)

SECTION III - THE BUILDING ITSELF

REGIONALITY

Over the course of history, the environment has been the strongest determinant of what form shelter will take. In order to be successful, a shelter must be built to counter local negative environmental conditions, and it must be constructed with available materials. These two factors are chiefly responsible for the distinctly regional quality of pre-industrial indigenous architecture. This section of the book examines the materials and techniques that builders used to achieve the goals mentioned in the previous sections.

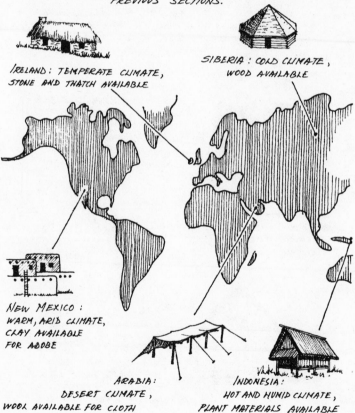

IRELAND: TEMPERATE CLIMATE, STONE AND THATCH AVAILABLE

SIBERIA: COLD CLIMATE, WOOD AVAILABLE

NEW MEXICO: WARM, ARID CLIMATE, CLAY AVAILABLE FOR ADOBE

ARABIA: DESERT CLIMATE, WOOL AVAILABLE FOR CLOTH

INDONESIA: HOT AND HUMID CLIMATE, PLANT MATERIALS AVAILABLE

PALM FRONDS AND GRASS SUPPLY
WEAVERBIRDS WITH THE
MATERIALS NECESSARY TO
CREATE THEIR INTRICATELY
WOVEN, SPHERICAL
NESTS.

THE EARLIEST MAN-MADE SHELTER
WAS MOST LIKELY A ROOF OF STICKS,
BRANCHES, AND LEAVES BRIDGING A
TROUGH IN THE TERRAIN.

THIS ABORIGINAL SHELTER
IN CENTRAL AUSTRALIA
IS MADE OF ARCHED
BRANCHES WITH A LEAF
COVERING. THE FLOOR
IS SLIGHTLY SCOOPED OUT.

THE BAMBUTI PEOPLE
OF THE ITURI FOREST IN THE
CONGO USE LARGE LEAVES TO
COVER TWIG FRAMES AS A
SIMPLE SHELTER.

THE DINKA TRIBE
OF THE UPPER NILE
USES SOME LOCAL
MATERIALS IN PLACE.
THE TWIG AND
THATCH ROOF OF THIS
HUT IS SUPPORTED
BY THE TRIMMED BRANCHES
OF A TREE.

ON LAKE TITICACA, IN PERU, THE URUS INDIANS HAVE USED TOTORA REEDS TO CREATE FLOATING ISLANDS UPON WHICH THEY BUILD THEIR HOUSES. THE HOUSES THEMSELVES ARE ALSO BUILT ENTIRELY OF REEDS.

THIS PRIMITIVE AUSTRALIAN HUT IS MADE OF LARGE SHEETS OF BARK BENT OVER A SIMPLE STICK FRAME.

FOR CENTURIES, THE JAPANESE HAVE BEEN DISPLAYING THEIR MASTERY OF THE CRAFT OF THATCHING.

TAKAYAMA, JAPAN

THE BOUND BUNDLES OF STRAW CAN BE MADE INTO ROOFS (ABOVE) OR WALLS (LEFT). THATCH IS USED THROUGHOUT THE WORLD BECAUSE GRASS IS SO UNIVERSALLY AVAILABLE AND IS REPLENISHABLE.

IN NORWAY, SOD HAS LONG BEEN USED AS A DURABLE, INSULATING ROOF MATERIAL. IT IS OFTEN PLACED OVER A LAYER OF BARK, WHICH KEEPS WATER FROM SEEPING INTO THE HOUSE.

SOD
BARK
WOOD
SECTION THROUGH ROOF

LOG HOUSE
WITH
SOD ROOF

OSTERDAL, NORWAY (17ᵗʰ CENTURY)

THE WELL-DIGGER JAWFISH
BUILDS A HIDEAWAY FROM WHICH TO
STRIKE AT PREY BY DIGGING A HOLE
AND REINFORCING IT WITH
PEBBLES AND SHELLS.

PERHAPS THE EARLIEST
FORM OF MAN-MADE STONE
BUILDING IS THE DOLMEN:
A STRUCTURE OF STONE
SLABS USED AS A
BURIAL CHAMBER.

THIS PRE-DYNASTIC EGYPTIAN
HOUSE WAS CREATED WITHIN
A BOULDER FORMATION.

THIS TRULLO DWELLING
IS BUILT OF UNMORTARED
STONE, WHICH IS CORBELED
TO CREATE A VAULTED
INTERIOR.

MURGIA, ITALY
(CA. 1600)

THE MOST WIDELY AVAILABLE
BUILDING MATERIAL IS THE
EARTH ITSELF. FOR MILLIONS
OF YEARS, ANIMALS HAVE
BEEN LIVING IN BURROWS
FOR PROTECTION FROM
COLD, HEAT, MOISTURE,
AND PREDATORS.
MANY BURROWS ARE
EVEN EQUIPPED WITH
SHORT TUNNELS USED AS
BATHROOMS.

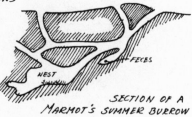

SECTION OF A
MARMOT'S SUMMER BURROW

3,000 YEARS AGO, PEOPLE
CARVED BURIAL CHAM-
BERS INTO THESE
CLIFFS OF SOFT ROCK.
DURING THE MIDDLE
AGES THEY WERE
CONVERTED INTO
DWELLINGS.

CARVED CLIFF HOUSES, ANAPO VALLEY, SICILY

IN NORTHERN CHINA, A
VERY LARGE NUMBER OF
PEOPLE LIVE IN SUBTERRA-
NEAN DWELLINGS CARVED
INTO THE LOESS SOIL AND
RADIATING FROM SUNKEN
COURTYARDS.

UNDERGROUND DWELLINGS
NEAR LO-YANG, NO. CHINA

MANY ELABORATE, MULTI-
LEVEL DWELLINGS HAVE
BEEN CARVED FROM THE
SOFT TUFA CONES OF
CAPPADOCIA.

CAPPADOCIA, TURKEY

ANOTHER WAY TO USE
EARTH FOR SHELTER IS
TO CUT SOD BLOCKS
AND USE THEM LIKE
BRICKS TO BUILD
WALLS.

SOD HOUSE
AMERICAN MIDWEST
(CA. 1840)

THE ANIMALS HUNTED
BY THE PLAINS INDIANS
SUPPLIED THEM WITH
FOOD AND SHELTER.
THE DEMOUNTABLE POLE
FRAMES OF THEIR TEPEES
ARE COVERED INSIDE
AND OUT WITH
HIDES.

AMERICAN PLAINS INDIAN TEPEE

THE TEKNA TRIBES OF SOUTHWEST
MOROCCO USE THE HAIR
FROM SHEEP, GOATS, AND
CAMELS AS THE RAW
MATERIAL FOR THEIR
TENTS. THESE PORTABLE
AND EASILY ERECTED
TENTS ARE WELL SUITED TO
THE TEKNA'S NOMADIC
LIFESTYLE.

TEKNA TENT
MOROCCO

IN A SUB-ARCTIC CLIMATE,
SNOW IS ONE OF THE FEW
MATERIALS AVAILABLE.
MANY TRIBES HAVE USED
SNOW BLOCKS IN CON-
STRUCTION FOR CENTURIES.
THE BLOCKS, EASILY CUT
AND SHAPED, ARE LAID IN
A SPIRALING PATTERN.

INUIT IGLOO
CANADA

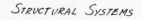

OUR PALEOLITHIC ANCESTORS MIGHT HAVE TAKEN REFUGE IN SOME NATURAL LEAN-TO SHELTERS OF TREES FALLEN AGAINST A BANK OR ACCROSS A GULLY.

LATER, THEY LEARNED HOW TO BUILD THEM THEMSELVES.

THE NEXT STEP MAY HAVE BEEN A LEAN-TO ROOF RESTING ON A CROSSBAR.

THE MORE COMMON, CIRCULAR DWELLING MAY HAVE ORIGINATED WITH A LEAN-TO RADIATING FROM A TREE.

NEOLITHIC MAN BUILT PITHOUSES THAT HAD A CIRCULAR FRAME ROOF OVER A SHALLOW PIT.

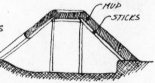

MUD
STICKS

PITHOUSE, PAN-P'O, CHINA (4000 B.C.)

THE RECTANGULAR PITHOUSE WAS A MORE RATIONAL FORM; THE CIRCULAR WAS MORE INTUITIVE.

TENCHI-GONGEN PITHOUSE, JAPAN

THE NEXT PHASE WAS THE DIFFER-ENTIATION OF WALL AND ROOF.

WOODEN CRUCK

ENGLISH CRUCK BUILDING (1500)

97

STONE STRUCTURES

STONE
EARTH

MORTARLESS STONE VAULTING
APPEARED IN EGYPT AND MESOPOTAMIA
BEFORE 3000 B.C. AND WAS OF THE
CORBELED, TRULLO TYPE.

CORBELED
STONEWORK

TRULLO HOUSE, MURGIA, ITALY (1400's)

THE AEGEAN CULTURES
OF GREECE AND CRETE MADE
EXTENSIVE USE OF THE STONE
LINTEL BECAUSE OF THE
DURABLE STONE AVAILABLE
TO THEM.

STONE LINTEL, GREECE

THE TRIANGULAR ARCH MARKED A TRANSITION
FROM THE LINTEL TO THE ARCH.

WINDOW LINTEL, TIGRÉ HOUSE
ETHIOPIA

VAULTED, UNMORTARED
STONE STRUCTURES
APPEARED IN
EUROPE ALSO.

STONE ORATORY, IRELAND
(6ᵗʰ OR 7ᵗʰ CENTURY)

A COMMON BUILDING TYPE IS A
MIXTURE OF MASSIVE STONE
WALLS AND A LIGHT, EASILY
CONSTRUCTED FRAME AND
THATCH ROOF.

FARMHOUSE, SCOTLAND (18ᵗʰ CENTURY)

VAULTS AND DOMES

THE STICKLEBACK FISH BUILDS A VAULTED NEST BY CONSTRUCTING A SOLID, SEMI-CYLINDRICAL MASS OF PLANT MATERIAL AND THEN TUNNELING A HOLE THROUGH IT.

FOR CENTURIES, VARIOUS CULTURES HAVE USED PLANT MATERIALS TO FRAME AND COVER VAULTS.

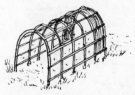

INDIAN FRAME VAULT, AMERICA

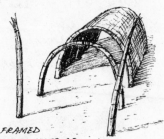

VAULT FRAMED WITH JOINED BUNDLES OF REEDS AND COVERED WITH REED MATS, IRAQ

MORE RECENTLY, CONCRETE HAS BEEN USED TO BUILD THIN-SHELLED VAULTS

AIRSHIP HANGAR, FRANCE (1916)

CONTEMPORARY DOMES ARE OFTEN OF PRECAST CONCRETE SECTIONS BOUND BY A BAND, OR TENSION RING, AROUND THE PERIMETER.

CONCRETE DOME, VIRGINIA (1964)

A VERY ANCIENT, INTUITIVE HOUSE FORM IS THE DOME, OR BEEHIVE SHAPE.

KHOISAN HUT SOUTH AFRICA

POST AND LINTEL

IT IS EASY TO SEE HOW THE LATER GREEK MONUMENTAL ARCHITECTURE EVOLVED FROM THIS SIMPLE, PRIMITIVE HUT, WHICH HAS TREE TRUNK POSTS AND TIMBER ROOF FRAMING.

GREEK HUT (PRE- 3000 B.C.)

THE CAPITAL ATOP EACH COLUMN SPREADS THE SUPPORT OF THE COLUMN ALONG THE ARCHITRAVE.

ARCHITRAVE →

CAPITAL { ABACUS
ECHINUS

COLUMN →

ANCIENT EXAMPLES OF STONE CONSTRUCTION USING MASSIVE LINTEL BLOCKS CAN BE FOUND THROUGHOUT CENTRAL AND SOUTH AMERICA.

MACHU PICCHU, PERU (CA.1500)

WHERE POSTS AND BEAMS ARE USED IN PUEBLO ARCHITECTURE, A ZAPATA IS USUALLY ADDED, LIKE A CAPITAL, TO SPREAD THE SUPPORT OF THE POST.

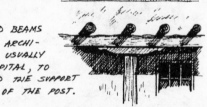

SANTA FE, NEW MEXICO (CA. 1860)

IN HOLLAND, WOOD POST AND BEAM CONSTRUCTION IS USED TO SUPPORT MASONRY WALLS WHILE PROVIDING LARGE OPENINGS FOR STORE WINDOWS.

AMSTERDAM, HOLLAND (CA. 1850)

THE FRAME

A FRAME STRUCTURAL
SYSTEM WITH A SKIN OF ROOF AND
WALLS HAS SEVERAL ADVANTAGES
OVER SOLID BUILDINGS. IT IS
LIGHTER, CAN BE ASSEMBLED
MORE QUICKLY, IS OFTEN DEMOUNT-
ABLE, USES MATERIALS MORE ECO-
NOMICALLY, IS EASY TO ALTER AND
EXPAND, AND CAN FLEX TO
RESIST EARTHQUAKES.

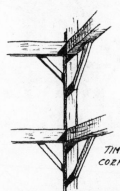

FRAME OF
BOUND POLES
VENEZUELA

MURO-JI SHRINE
JAPAN

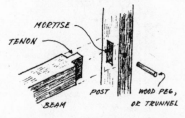

MORTISE

TENON

POST

BEAM

WOOD PEG,
OR TRUNNEL

MORTISE AND TENON JOINT

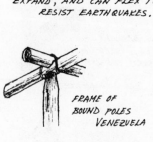

TIMBER FRAME WITH
CORNER BRACING

THE CORNER BRACING HELPS A
FRAME STRUCTURE TO RESIST LATERAL
FORCES SUCH AS WIND AND
EARTHQUAKES (SEE PAGE 25).

THE HALF-TIMBER STRUCTURE
HAS WALLS OF STONE, BRICK, PLASTER,
OR WATTLE AND DAUB (SEE PAGE 121), WHICH
FILL IN THE AREAS BETWEEN THE TIMBERS,
LEAVING THEM EXPOSED.

HALF-TIMBER HOUSE, DENMARK

THE CANTILEVER

THIS OVERHANGING, OR JETTIED, SECOND FLOOR ADDS SPACE UPSTAIRS AND ALSO PRO- TECTS THE LOWER WALL FROM THE WEATHER.

KENT, ENGLAND
(15ᵗʰ CENTURY)

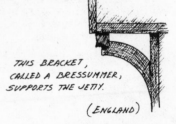

THIS BRACKET, CALLED A BRESSUMMER, SUPPORTS THE JETTY.

(ENGLAND)

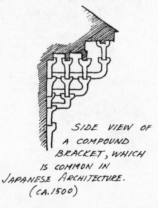

SIDE VIEW OF A COMPOUND BRACKET, WHICH IS COMMON IN JAPANESE ARCHITECTURE.
(CA. 1500)

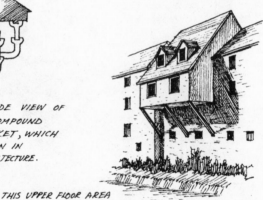

THIS UPPER FLOOR AREA IS CANTILEVERED OVER A RIVER AND IS SUPPORTED BY DIAGONAL BRACES.

LUXEMBOURG

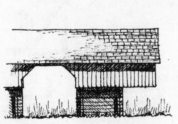

OVERSHOT BARN; TENNESSEE

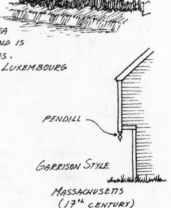

PENDILL

GARRISON STYLE

MASSACHUSETTS
(17ᵗʰ CENTURY)

Molded Structures

The potter wasp builds small clay pots to protect its eggs. It gathers small balls of clay, which it moistens, fashions into flat, narrow strips, and uses to build up the wall of the pot. It then lays an egg inside suspended over a collection of paralyzed insects that will be food for the larva. The top is then corked with a ball of clay. When the young wasp is large enough, it breaks out of its pot.

Potter wasp clay pots

Semi-spherical clay hut Afghanistan

The round mud hut of the Massa tribe in the Sudan is built of successive courses of mud, laid and shaped by hand, forming a cylinder and topped with a thatch roof.

Massa mud hut Logone River Sudan

Some structures built by the Hohokam Indians of Arizona were constructed by building up courses of hand-shaped mud two to three feet high.

Casa Grande, Arizona (ca. 1250)

The Spanish technique of using board forms to hold the poured wall while it cured was used in the construction of Tabby walls. (See page 71.)

Tabby wall St. Augustine, Florida (1750)

THE ROOF

Perhaps the first man-made roof form was the lean-to. It is a simple, intuitive answer to the need for shelter.

"Banab," or rain shelter, of the Southern Guiana Indians (the frame gets a cover of brush.)

One of the earliest and simplest roof forms is the cone. Of all the shapes that can be built using straight members, the conical roof offers a maximum of floor area with a minimum of exposed surface area.

Penobscot Indian Tepee

Usable living space can be increased when the conical roof is raised on outer walls.

Wai Wai Dwelling British Guiana

This example shows an interesting combination of gable and conical roofs. The gable allows for a large interior space and the conical ends minimize surface exposure there.

Jibaru Jivaria, Ecuador

The gable roof allows for better through-ventilation and also permits easy linear expansion of the structure. (A circle is more difficult to expand than a rectangle.)

Seminole Lodge

IN SIMPLE, PRIMITIVE
DWELLINGS THERE IS NO
DIFFERENTIATION BETWEEN
THE ROOF AND THE WALLS.

CHURUATA HUT
VENEZUELA

THE CHURUATA HUT OF THE VENEZUELAN INDIANS IS MADE BY PLACING A CIRCLE OF POLES IN THE GROUND, THEN BENDING THEM INTO A DOUBLE CURVE AND BINDING THEM AT THE TOP.

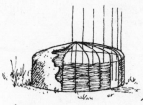

THE MASAI BUILD THEIR HUTS IN A SIMILAR WAY EXCEPT THAT TWIGS, WOVEN BETWEEN THE SAPLING POLES, CREATE A VERTICAL WALL, ABOVE WHICH THE SAPLINGS ARE BENT TO ARC ACROSS TO THE OTHER SIDE.
THE HOUSE IS LATER PLASTERED WITH A MIXTURE OF MUD AND DUNG.

MASAI HOUSE
AFRICA

THE ADDED SUPPORTING POLES AROUND THE PERIMETER OF THIS HOUSE SUGGEST THE BEGINNINGS OF A SEPARATE WALL SYSTEM.

WICHITA INDIAN HOUSE

MARQUESAS Is.
HOUSE

IN THIS HOUSE, THE WALL STRUCTURE IS PLAINLY SEPARATED FROM THE ROOF. THIS RESULTS IN THE ELIMINATION OF THE THE UNUSABLE LOW-CEILINGED SPACE AT THE PERIMETER.

HOUSE FORMS THAT AVOID THE TRANSITION FROM WALL TO ROOF ARE STILL POPULAR TODAY BECAUSE THEY ARE EASY TO BUILD, USE FEWER MATERIALS, AND OFFER GOOD PROTECTION FROM THE WEATHER.

A-FRAME HOUSE, VERMONT

WOOD ROOF STRUCTURES

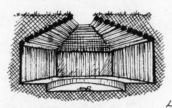

SECTION THROUGH LOG DOME
MESA VERDE, COLORADO

WHERE AVAILABLE, WOOD HAS ALWAYS BEEN A POPULAR BUILDING MATERIAL BECAUSE IT IS EASY TO SHAPE AND IS RELATIVELY LIGHT. IN SOME PRIMITIVE BUILDINGS IT WAS LAID IN COURSES OR CORBELED LIKE STONEWORK.

LOG DOME, PAKISTAN
(VIEWED FROM BELOW)

BECAUSE OF ITS FIBROUS NATURE, WOOD IS ABLE TO RESIST BENDING FORCES BETTER THAN MATERIALS SUCH AS STONE, WHICH FRACTURE EASILY. FOR THIS REASON, WOOD HAS BEEN FAVORED FOR CENTURIES AS A GOOD MATERIAL TO SPAN THE LIVING SPACE AND SUPPORT THE WEIGHT OF THE ROOF AND SNOW.

BENDING FORCE

MANDAN HOUSE, AMERICAN NORTHERN
PLAINS

PREHISTORIC PIT HOUSE
WITH POLE ROOF

HOUSE FRAME
PENNSYLVANIA
(CA. 1700)

THE SAME FRAMING SYSTEM USED IN THE PREHISTORIC PITHOUSE ABOVE IS THE MOST COMMON ROOF CONSTRUCTION TECHNIQUE USED TODAY. IT CONSISTS OF RAFTERS SPANNING FROM THE WALL SILL OR BEAM TO THE RIDGE. MODERN FRAMING USUALLY INCLUDES A BOARD AT THE RIDGE.

VAULTED AND DOMED ROOFS

IN AREAS WHERE HEAVY TIMBER WAS NOT AVAILABLE FOR USE AS STRAIGHT ROOF BEAMS THE VAULT AROSE AS A SUBSTITUTE. BY SIMPLY SECURING ONE END OF A SAPLING, BENDING IT, AND SECURING THE OTHER END ONE CAN CREATE AN ARCH. A SERIES OF THESE FORMS A VAULT. IT IS NO SURPRISE THAT THIS IS, PERHAPS, THE MOST WIDESPREAD ROOF FORM.

VAULTED HOUSE
CAREENING BAY, AUSTRALIA

ALTERNATIVE MATERIALS, SUCH AS STONE, CLAY, OR BRICK, ARE STRONG WHEN BEING COMPRESSED BUT WEAK WHEN BEING BENT. A HORIZONTAL ROOF BEAM EXPERIENCES BENDING, BUT IN A VAULT OR DOME ALL THE ELEMENTS ARE UNDER COMPRESSION, SO IT IS A FORM THAT IS PARTICULARLY SUITED TO THOSE MATERIALS.

BARREL VAULTED HOUSES
GREECE

THIS STRUCTURE, CALLED A "CASELLA," HAS AN INNER CORBELED STONE DOME COVERED WITH EARTH AND AN OUTER STONE SURFACE.

"CASELLA"; APULIA, ITALY

CONICAL DOMED ROOF
OF HAND-MOLDED CLAY

NORTHERN CAMEROON

MUD BRICK
SAIL VAULTS BUILT ON
RUBBLE STONE WALLS

CARAVANSARAI; QUM, IRAN

TRUSSES

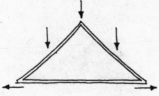

IN A SIMPLE GABLE ROOF, THE DOWNWARD FORCES FROM THE WEIGHT OF THE ROOFING AND ANY SNOW WILL CAUSE BENDING IN THE RAFTERS AND EXERT AN OUTWARD FORCE AT THE BASE OF THE ROOF.

TRUSSES GIVE THE RAFTERS ADDITIONAL BRACING AND TIE THE BASE OF THE ROOF TOGETHER SO THAT IT DOESN'T SPREAD AND COLLAPSE.

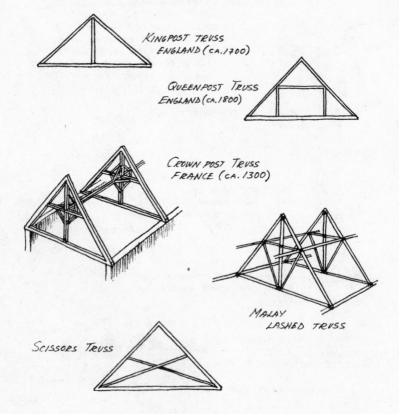

KINGPOST TRUSS
ENGLAND (CA. 1700)

QUEENPOST TRUSS
ENGLAND (CA. 1800)

CROWN POST TRUSS
FRANCE (CA. 1300)

MALAY
LASHED TRUSS

SCISSORS TRUSS

ROOFING MATERIALS

VEGETAL ROOFS:

ROOF OF PALM LEAVES
LAID SHINGLE STYLE

JOHORE, MALAYSIA

KIRDI HUT WITH ROOF
OF PILED GRASS

MULTI-LAYER, BUILT-UP
THATCH ROOF
SUDAN

THATCHED COTTAGE
FRANCE (CA.1885)

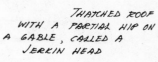

THATCHED ROOF
WITH A PARTIAL HIP ON
A GABLE, CALLED A
JERKIN HEAD

HAMPSHIRE, ENGLAND

THATCH:

VIEW OF UNDERSIDE OF REED AND
THATCH ROOF WITH BAMBOO
RAFTERS

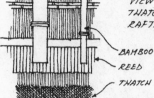

KATSURA, JAPAN
(CA. 1630)

BAMBOO
REED
THATCH

SECTION THROUGH
BAMBOO SUPPORTED
THATCH ROOF (JAPAN)

BAMBOO

STEEP ROOFS DIVERT
HEAVY, TROPICAL RAINS

ROCK
FOUNDATION

GRASS THATCH HUTS
INSIDE A STONE ENCLOSURE
(MARQUESAS ISLANDS)

SECTION THROUGH ROOF
SHOWING OVERLAP ON
STONE WALL

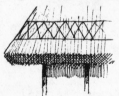

ROPE STITCHING TO PREVENT WIND FROM
LIFTING THE THATCH
SUSSEX, ENGLAND
(CA. 1699)

HAT-LIKE CAPS ON
THATCHED ROOFS GIVE
ACCESS TO GRANARIES.

DORMER WINDOWS IN A
THATCHED ROOF

KENT, ENGLAND

STONE ROOFS

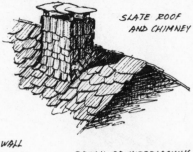

SLATE ROOF
AND CHIMNEY

STONE ROOF AND WALL
BORGONE, ITALY

DETAIL OF INTERLOCKING
SLATES AT THE ROOF RIDGE

PENALBA DE SANTIAGO,
SPAIN

SLATE ROOF
WITH TERRA-COTTA
TILE TO SEAL THE RIDGE

CHAMONIX, FRANCE

SLATE ROOF WITH
ROCKS TO PREVENT
WIND DAMAGE

SWITZERLAND

SOME CUT SLATE
PATTERNS

SQUARED

BEVELED

DIAMOND

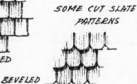

OUTER ROOF

EARTH

THE TRULLO STRUCTURES
OF APULIA HAVE AN INNER
STONE VAULT AND AN OUTER
ROOF OF STONES THAT ARE SLIGHTLY
TILTED TO DIVERT WATER.

APULIA, ITALY

111

TILE ROOFS

PANTILE ROOF
NETHERLANDS (17th CENTURY)

MISSION
TILE

MEXICO (CA. 1800)

MISSION TILE ROOF
MEXICO

DETAIL OF
CEMENTED JOINT AT
THE RIDGE

TILED GABLE AND SHED ROOFS
PROVENCE, FRANCE

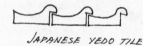

JAPANESE YEDO TILE

TILES AT THE
EAVES HAVE
AN ORNAMENTAL
DESIGN.

TILED HOUSE, HAKODATE,
JAPAN (CA. 1880)

VAULTED ROOF UNDER
CONSTRUCTION; NOTE THE
RECTANGULAR BRICK-LIKE
TILE BLOCKS.

TUNISIA

Wooden Roofs

In areas where tree bark can be harvested in large sheets, it is often used as a roofing material. In this example, poles secure the bark.

BARK COVERED HUT
NEW ENGLAND INDIANS
(CA. 1600)

THICK SLABS OF BARK CAN also be used like mission tiles (see page 112).

Logs themselves have sometimes been used for roofing, as in the scoop-log roof (right), or the split log roof (left).

SCOOP-LOG ROOF

SPLIT LOG ROOF
HELSINKI, FINLAND

ROOF OF
HAND-SPLIT SHAKES
NORTH CAROLINA
(CA. 1750)

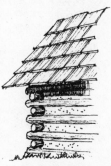

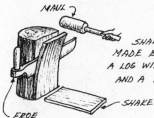

Shakes are made by splitting a log with a froe and a maul.

MAUL

FROE

SHAKE

ROOF OF SHAPED BOARDS
HORIUJI, JAPAN

BOARD ROOF, OR
"HISASHI"

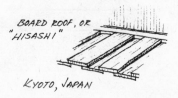

KYOTO, JAPAN

LOG HOUSE WITH SHINGLE ROOF
CZECHOSLOVAKIA (1903)

FOR WEATHER
PROTECTION, THE
NEXT BEST THING TO
DIGGING INTO THE
EARTH IS TO PILE
EARTH ON TOP.

SOD-ROOFED CABIN
COPENHAGEN, DENMARK

WHEN PROPERLY PACKED AND FINISHED, AND KEPT
FREE OF STANDING WATER, A ROOF MADE
FROM MUD CAN BE IMPERVIOUS TO RAIN
AND CAN INSULATE THE DWELLING.

HERRINGBONE PATTERN
OF CEILING BOARDS
SUPPORTING AN
ADOBE ROOF.

SAN ANTONIO,
TEXAS (CA. 1860)

ADOBE ROOF

ADOBE

GRASS AND
TWIGS

LOG BEAM

TAOS, NEW MEXICO
(CA. 1600)

STICK AND
POLE STRUCTURAL
SYSTEM SUPPORTING A
ROOF OF CALICHE, A SOIL WITH
A HIGH LIME CONTENT.

CASA GRANDE, ARIZONA (CA. 1250)

WHITEWASH
MUD
TWIG MAT
LOG BEAM

ROOF SYSTEM
PAKISTAN

NEBRASKA SODDIE (CA. 1886)

THE BUILDERS OF THE
SOD HOUSES OF THE
PLAINS STATES USED
SOD TO CONSTRUCT THE
WALLS AND ALSO AS A
COVERING FOR THE
WOOD ROOF.

THE CUBITERMES TERMITES USE SOIL PARTICLES CEMENTED WITH EXCREMENT TO BUILD THEIR LARGE, MUSHROOM-SHAPED COLONIES. THE DOMED ROOF ACTS LIKE AN UMBRELLA TO DIVERT THE HEAVY TROPICAL RAINS.

CUBITERMES COLONY

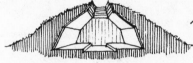

ALASKAN ESKIMO WINTER HOUSE WITH EARTH COVERING

FRONT ELEVATION

ONLY THE TWO SMALL GABLE ENDS OF THIS EARTH-COVERED HOUSE ARE EXPOSED TO THE WEATHER.

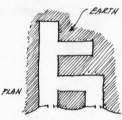

EARTH

PLAN

GREECE (1876)

MANY OF THE OLD BUILDINGS IN ICELAND HAVE THEIR WALLS PROTECTED FROM THE COLD BY LARGE MASSES OF EARTH. BLOCKS OF TURF ARE COURSED IN A HERRINGBONE PATTERN AND ALSO CARRIED UP OVER THE ROOF.

OLD CHURCH ICELAND

CONTEMPORARY EARTH-SHELTERED HOUSE LYME, NEW HAMPSHIRE

OTHER ROOFING MATERIALS:

SKINS:

INUIT "TUPIQ"
THE INUIT SUMMER DWELLING,
OR "TUPIQ," IS MADE FROM SEAL-
SKINS STRETCHED OVER A WOODEN
FRAME AND HELD SECURE BY GUY
ROPES AND ROCKS AROUND THE
PERIMETER.

PLAINS INDIAN TEPEE
A SKIN MEMBRANE IS
ATTACHED TO BOTH THE
INSIDE AND THE OUTSIDE
OF THE POLES.

FABRIC:

MOOR TENT FROM MAURETANIA
FABRIC MADE OF GOAT HAIR IS STRETCHED
OVER A FEW POLES AND STAKED WITH
THE OPENING DOWN WIND.

YURT FROM KIRGHIZISTAN
MULTI-LAYER GOAT HAIR FABRIC IS
TIED OVER A WOODEN FRAME.

METAL:

TIN ROOF
ELKHORN, MONTANA (CA. 1890)
IT WENT UP QUICKLY BUT
WAS A POOR INSULATOR.

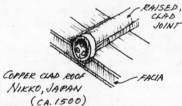

RAISED,
CLAD
JOINT

FACIA

COPPER CLAD ROOF
NIKKO, JAPAN
(CA. 1500)
IT WEATHERS WELL AND
TAKES ON A NICE PATINA.

OTHER:

DULLES AIRPORT, VIRGINIA
CABLE-SUPPORTED CONCRETE ROOF

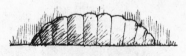

AIR-SUPPORTED TENNIS COURT
ENCLOSURE OF SYNTHETIC
FABRIC, BOSTON

THE WALL

As the wall became a separate structure from the roof it also took on separate functions. Beyond insulating the house, the roof is built to keep out rain, snow, and sun, while the primitive wall deals with wind, animals, and neighbors.

In its simplest form, the wall is a light vegetal membrane that offers privacy, shade, and protection from wind and rain.

BAMBOO AND REED WALL
FIJI ISLANDS

AÏR - TUAREG TENT
WITH MOVABLE WALLS OF
WOVEN STRAW

WOVEN WALLS OFFER SHADE AND RAIN PROTECTION BUT ALLOW SOME AIR FLOW, WHICH IS ESSENTIAL IN HUMID CLIMATES.

HERRINGBONE WEAVE

UPPER VOLTA

WALL OF SAPLINGS LAID BETWEEN PAIRS OF PERIMETER POSTS

POKOT DWELLING KENYA

STILT HOUSE WITH SPLIT BAMBOO WALLS

ROLL-DOWN WOVEN WALL PANELS

GILBERT ISLANDS

SOUTH DAHOMEY

THE LOG WALL

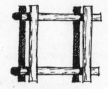

THE INSULATING PROPERTIES OF SOLID WOOD AND THE PREVALENCE OF FORESTS IN COOLER CLIMATES PROMOTE LOG WALL CONSTRUCTION IN THOSE AREAS.

PLAN OF A "SRUB"

RUSSIA HAS SOME OF THE EARLIEST LOG STRUCTURES. THEY ARE BASED ON A UNIT CALLED A "SRUB," A SIMPLE SQUARE FORMED BY FOUR TREE TRUNKS. THE NOREGIANS EXTENDED THE SIDES BY JOINING SEVERAL LOGS END-TO-END.

CROSS SECTIONS OF COMMON LOG TREATMENTS:

 RUSSIAN (UNTRIMMED)

 NORWEGIAN (2 SIDES SQUARED)

 ALPINE (4 SIDES SQUARED)

YUKAGHIR LOG HOUSE WITH A SOD ROOF SIBERIA

LOG CABIN WITH CHINKING TO SEAL THE GAP BETWEEN THE LOGS.

INDIANA (CA. 1850)

YAKUT VERTICAL LOG WALL WITH COVERING OF MUD

SIBERIA

LOG STOREHOUSE ALVROS, SWEDEN (CA. 1753)

THE MORE PRIMITIVE LOG
JOINTS ARE MADE BY
CUTTING A SMALL SADDLE
OUT OF THE TOP AND
BOTTOM OF
EACH LOG.

V-NOTCH

SADDLE JOINT

SHAPING THE LOG SO
THAT IT HAS A PEAKED UPPER
SURFACE AND CUTTING V-NOTCHES
IN THE BOTTOM CREATES A
JOINT THAT WILL REDUCE ROT,
BECAUSE IT DOES NOT
TRAP WATER.

HEWN LOGS
WITH A
SADDLE
NOTCH

THIS JOINT COMBINES THE
SIMPLICITY OF THE SADDLE JOINT WITH
THE DRAINING ADVANTAGE OF
THE V-NOTCH.

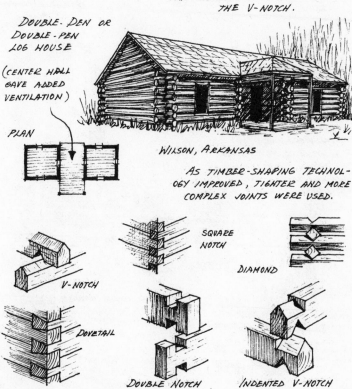

DOUBLE-DEN OR
DOUBLE-PEN
LOG HOUSE

(CENTER HALL
GAVE ADDED
VENTILATION)

PLAN

WILSON, ARKANSAS

AS TIMBER-SHAPING TECHNOL-
OGY IMPROVED, TIGHTER AND MORE
COMPLEX JOINTS WERE USED.

SQUARE
NOTCH

DIAMOND

V-NOTCH

DOVETAIL

DOUBLE NOTCH

INDENTED V-NOTCH

Wood Walls

ADVANCES IN WOOD SAWING AND MILLING TECHNOLOGY GREATLY REFINED THE WOOD FRAMING SYSTEMS AND ALSO BROUGHT ABOUT THE EXTENSIVE USE OF SAWN BOARDS AS A SIDING MATERIAL. A VARIETY OF TYPES AROSE IN AN EFFORT TO CREATE A TIGHT WALL WITH ROT-RESISTANT JOINTS.

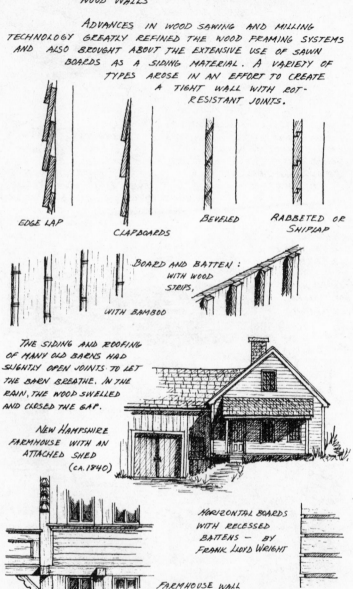

EDGE LAP

CLAPBOARDS

BEVELED

RABBETED OR SHIPLAP

BOARD AND BATTEN:
WITH WOOD STRIPS,

WITH BAMBOO

THE SIDING AND ROOFING OF MANY OLD BARNS HAD SLIGHTLY OPEN JOINTS TO LET THE BARN BREATHE. IN THE RAIN, THE WOOD SWELLED AND CLOSED THE GAP.

NEW HAMPSHIRE FARMHOUSE WITH AN ATTACHED SHED (CA. 1840)

HORIZONTAL BOARDS WITH RECESSED BATTENS — BY FRANK LLOYD WRIGHT

FARMHOUSE WALL BERN, SWITZERLAND

WATTLE AND DAUB

THE USE OF MUD PLASTER (DAUB) OVER A MATRIX OF WOOD, REED, OR BAMBOO STRIPS (WATTLE) TO BUILD WALLS ACTUALLY PREDATES THE EGYPTIAN CULTURE.

WATTLE AND DAUB WALL

HUNGARIAN PEASANT HOUSE

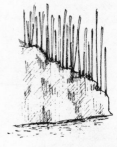

THE EARLIEST FORM OF MUD-PLASTERED WALL CONSTRUCTION WAS PROBABLY JACAL (MUD OVER VERTICAL PIECES PLANTED IN THE GROUND).

JACAL WALL, KEET SEEL, NAVAHO NATIONAL MONUMENT, ARIZONA

HORIZONTAL WOOD STRIPS LASHED TO POSTS AND THEN PLASTERED WITH MUD THAT HAS BEEN MIXED WITH STRAW TO HOLD IT TOGETHER

VENEZUELA

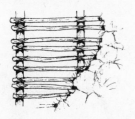

THE BAMBOO MESH IN THIS WALL HAS BEEN LEFT UNPLASTERED IN ONE SECTION TO LEAVE A WINDOW WITH A GRILLE.

JAPAN

A MORE ADVANCED USE OF THE WATTLE AND DAUB IS IN HALF-TIMBER CONSTRUCTION. THE WATTLE IS FRAMED INTO THE TIMBER STRUCTURE, THEN PLASTERED, LEAVING THE TIMBERS EXPOSED.

ENGLAND

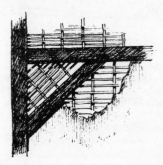

IN OTHER HALF-TIMBER
CONSTRUCTION, MASONRY
FILLS IN THE WALL AREA
BETWEEN THE TIMBERS.

BRICK INFILLED HALF-
TIMBER HOUSE
NEWGATE, YORK
ENGLAND (CA. 1380)

A VERY COMMON,
PRIMITIVE TYPE OF WALL
IS THAT OF HAND-FORMED
MUD COURSES.

NORTHERN IVORY COAST

COB (MUD MIXED WITH
STRAW FOR ADDED STRENGTH)
WAS A FAVORITE BUILDING
MATERIAL IN MANY PARTS
OF ENGLAND.

STONE ENDED COB HOUSE
DEVON, ENGLAND

WALLS OF TABBY, A MIXTURE
OF LIME, SAND, WATER, AND
AGGREGATE (BROKEN SHELLS),
ARE COMMON IN OLDER
HOMES IN THE SOUTHERN
U.S. THE WALLS WERE
FORMED BY POURING THE
TABBY BETWEEN FORM
BOARDS (SEE PAGE 103).

ST. AUGUSTINE, FLORIDA

SOME WASPS BUILD TUBULAR NESTS BY FASHIONING SMALL MUD CYLINDERS AND THEN LAYERING THEM TO CREATE THE ARCHED SHAPE OF THE NEST.

WASP'S NEST

FOR OVER 8,000 YEARS, CULTURES THE WORLD OVER HAVE BUILT WITH MUD BRICKS. THE SHAPING OF THE BRICKS WAS ORIGINALLY DONE BY HAND AND LATER WITH MOLDS. DURABILITY WAS INCREASED BY FIRING THEM.

BRICK AND MOLD
MALI

AFTER THE ARRIVAL OF THE SPANISH IN AMERICA THE PUEBLO INDIANS BEGAN BUILDING WITH ADOBE BRICKS RATHER THAN WITH HAND-SHAPED OR PUDDLED ADOBE.

PUEBLO DWELLING
NEW MEXICO (17TH CENTURY)

MUD BRICK WALL AND PANTILE ROOF VENEZUELA

BECAUSE OF THEIR SQUARE AND REGULAR SHAPE, BRICKS ARE OFTEN USED IN CONJUNCTION WITH STONE TO MAKE SOLID, SQUARE CORNERS, DOOR AND WINDOW JAMBS, FLAT OR ARCHED LINTELS, SILLS, AND CHIMNEYS.

FLINT COBBLE AND BRICK HOUSE
NORFOLK, ENGLAND

TUMBLED BRICKWORK
SERVES AS BOTH A
STRENGTHENING AND A
DECORATIVE ELEMENT.

PROVINCE DU NORD, FRANCE

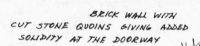

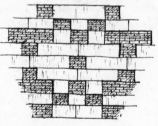

BRICK WALL WITH
CUT STONE QUOINS GIVING ADDED
SOLIDITY AT THE DOORWAY

VAL D'OISE, FRANCE

DECORATIVE WALL
TREATMENTS
COMBINING AREAS
OF STONE
AND BRICK

BRAY, FRANCE

NORMANDY,
FRANCE

A COMMON PRACTICE IS TO
REINFORCE THE CORNERS OF
BRICK STRUCTURES WITH
LARGE, CUT STONE
QUOINS.

BRICK, STONE, AND THATCH
HOUSE; TIDPIT
HAMPSHIRE, ENGLAND

AS WELL AS BEING AN
EFFICIENT WAY TO ENCLOSE
SPACE (SEE PAGE 27), THE
STONE BEEHIVE HUT DOES
NOT REQUIRE THE COMPLEX
FASHIONING OF
CORNERS IN STONE.

STONE AGE BEEHIVE HUT,
IRELAND

MASSIVE (NOTE SCALE
FIGURE) AND INTRICATELY
SHAPED AND FITTED STONES

SACSAHUAMAN, A STONE AGE
INDIAN FORTRESS; CUZCO, PERU

WHERE A VARIETY OF
STONE IS AVAILABLE, IT
OFTEN INSPIRES DECORATIVE
PATTERNS.

CHACO CANYON,
NEW MEXICO (CA. 1100)

SLATE AND BOULDERS
NORTHERN ENGLAND

WALLS OF GREEN SLATE
WITH QUOINS AND LINTELS OF
SLATE PLACED ON EDGE

ELTERWATER
CUMBRIA, ENGLAND

THE CORNICE, WINDOW JAMBS,
AND TRIANGULAR ARCH ARE
OF CUT STONE, WHILE THE
WALL IS OF SLATE WITH
BANDS OF RUBBLE STONE.

FRANCE

STONE SEGMENTAL ARCH
PENNSYLVANIA (18ᵀᴴ CENTURY)

PUEBLO BONITO (CA. 1050)

EXTENDED WOOD LINTEL
FOR ADDED TENSILE STRENGTH

CUT STONE LINTEL,
OR FLAT ARCH

ENGLAND (CA. 1618)

HOT SPRINGS, SOUTH DAKOTA (CA. 1891)

SQUARED BLOCKS,
CORNICEWORK, AND
SEMICIRCULAR
ARCHES - ALL
CUT FROM
LOCAL SANDSTONE.

TIGHT-FITTING
POLYGONAL
STONEWORK

KYOTO, JAPAN (CA. 1600)

IN EASTERN PORTUGAL SOME HOUSES HAVE A STONE WALL SYSTEM CONSISTING OF HUGE GRANITE SLABS AS MUCH AS TWELVE INCHES THICK SURROUNDED AND HELD IN PLACE BY SMALLER STONES.

GRANITE SLABS ARE ALSO USED FOR ROOFING AND PAVING.

WYTHES — BINDING STONE

TO MAKE A THICK, SOLID STONE WALL, SEVERAL TIERS, OR WYTHES, OF STONE ARE BUILT AND TIED TOGETHER AT INTERVALS WITH BINDING STONES. SOMETIMES THESE STONES PROTRUDE AND ARE USED AS SHELVES OR STAIRS.

THE INCA INDIANS OF PERU WERE ACCOMPLISHED STONE MASONS AND DEVELOPED THE TECHNIQUE OF USING COPPER CRAMPS TO HOLD STONES TOGETHER. THE METHOD THEY USED MAY HAVE BEEN TO POUR MOLTEN COPPER INTO PREPARED HOLES IN THE STONES.

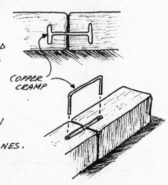

COPPER CRAMP

ANOTHER TECHNIQUE EMPLOYED BY THE INCAS WAS TO USE LONG STONES PRO- TRUDING FROM THE WALLS AS SUPPORTS FOR THE FLOOR JOISTS AND ROOF RAFTERS.

PERUVIAN ANDES
15ᵗʰ CENTURY

HYBRIDS:

A TRADEMARK OF INDIGENOUS ARCHITECTURE IS THE USE OF A VARIETY OF MATERIALS IN WAYS THAT TAKE BEST ADVANTAGE OF THEIR PARTICULAR PROPERTIES.

THE BUILDERS OF THIS PRIMITIVE, DECAYING HOUSE BUILT A SOLID FOUNDATION OF STONE, A LIGHT FRAME OF WOOD, A WATERPROOF ROOF OF THATCH, AND AN UPPER, WEATHERTIGHT WALL OF WATTLE AND DAUB.

THIS NORWEGIAN HOUSE HAS A FIRM STONE FOUNDATION, A SOLID FIRST-FLOOR BARN AND STORAGE AREA OF LOGS, AN UPPER LIVING AREA WITH TIMBER FRAMING AND LIGHT PLANK WALLS, AND AN INSULATING ROOF OF SOD OVER BARK.

A BARN IN HAGI, JAPAN WITH A MASSIVE STONE BASE, LOWER AND GABLE WALLS OF BOARDS OVER A TIMBER FRAME, OPEN-SLATTED WALL IN LOFT FOR VENTILATION, AND A TILE ROOF

AN OLD SWISS FARMHOUSE WITH LOWER WALLS OF STONE; OVER THAT, A TIMBER FRAME WITH WATTLE AND DAUB INFILL, AND A TILE ROOF WITH DEEP OVERHANGS

BERNESE FARMHOUSE SWITZERLAND

A GARDEN WALL WITH A COMBINATION OF STONE, EDGE-LAPPED BOARDS WITH EXTERIOR BATTENS, PLASTER OVER BAMBOO, AND TILE

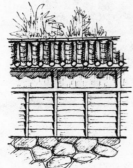

HAGI, JAPAN

POLE FRAME WITH ROCK INFILL AND PANTILE ROOF

GREECE

COTTAGE WITH STONE BASE, END WALLS, AND SEMICIRCULAR ARCHES, UPPER WALL OF HALF-TIMBER CONSTRUCTION, AND ROOF OF SHINGLES

JOSSELIN, FRANCE

THE EARLY SETTLERS IN THE AMERICAN MIDWEST HAD FEW BUILDING MATERIALS AVAILABLE SO THEY OFTEN USED BLOCKS OF SOD TO CONSTRUCT WALLS AND TO COVER THE ROOF.

SOD HOUSE; NEBRASKA (19ᵀᴴ CENTURY)

ANOTHER SIMPLE, EFFECTIVE, AND INEXPENSIVE SYSTEM IS THE STOVEWOOD WALL. IN WOODPILE FASHION THE LOGS ARE STACKED AND MORTARED LIKE STONEWORK. NOTE THE LOG QUOINS THAT REINFORCE THE CORNER.

STOVEWOOD WALL; CANADA

IN THE LATE NINETEENTH AND EARLY TWENTIETH CENTURIES TIN WAS USE EXTENSIVELY AS A CHEAP, WEATHER-RESISTANT COVERING FOR BARNS AND HOMES.

TIN SHINGLES AND PANELS MAINE

CEDAR SHINGLES HAVE BEEN WIDELY USED FOR CENTURIES AS BOTH A ROOF AND A WALL MATERIAL BECAUSE OF THEIR EXCELLENT WEATHER-RESISTANT QUALITIES.

SHINGLED HOUSE; HINGHAM, MASSACHUSETTS (1720)

BARN WITH WALLS
MADE OF BALES OF
HAY STAKED TOGETHER
AND ROOF MADE
OF STRAW

NEBRASKA (CA. 1910)

ENGLISH WALL TILES ARE LAPPED
LIKE SHINGLES, LEAVING
THE NAILS AND JOINTS
PROTECTED.

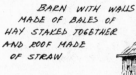

JAPANESE
FLAT TILES
ARE NAILED AT THE
CORNERS AND THEN THE
JOINTS ARE PLASTERED.

THE
BOTTLE
WALL

BOTTLES ARE LAID IN
MORTAR. THEY ADMIT
A BEAUTIFUL LIGHT
BUT INSULATE POORLY.

IN A SLIP-
FORMED STONE
WALL ROCKS ARE
PLACED BETWEEN
THE FORM BOARDS
AND CONCRETE IS
POURED. LATER,
THE FORM IS
SLIPPED UP TO HOLD
THE NEXT COURSE.

FORM BOARD

FORM
BRACE

IN MANY AREAS
SUBSTANTIAL HEATING CAN
BE SUPPLIED BY THE USE OF
GLASS ON THE SOUTH WALLS
TO TRAP SOLAR HEAT
INSIDE THE HOUSE.

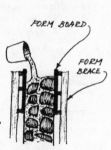

CONTEMPORARY PASSIVE SOLAR
HOUSE WITH ATTACHED GREENHOUSE
NEW LONDON, NEW HAMPSHIRE

THE FLOOR

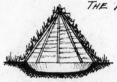

NEOLITHIC PIT HOUSE

THE SIMPLEST AND MOST COMMON FLOOR SURFACES FOUND IN PRIMITIVE DWELLINGS ARE OF PACKED EARTH AND ARE SOMETIMES COVERED WITH LEAVES, STRAW, SKINS, OR WOVEN MATS.

A FLOOR OF POURED MORTAR AND AGGREGATE MIXTURES, SUCH AS TABBY, GIVES A SURFACE THAT IS MORE DURABLE, CLEANER, AND DRIER. WHEN WORN, A NEW LAYER IS POURED ON TOP.

TABBY (2 IN.)

SHELLSTONE BASE (3 IN.)

ST. AUGUSTINE, FLORIDA (CA.1700)

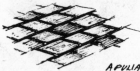

FLAT STONES ARE USED ALL OVER THE WORLD TO CREATE VERY DURABLE FLOORS AND PAVEMENTS.

APULIA, ITALY (CA.1600)

RIVED BOARD

EARLY WOOD FLOORS WERE OF RIVED BOARDS RESTING ON LOG JOISTS THAT HAD BEEN MADE FLAT ON THE UPPER SIDE WITH AN ADZE OR A BROADAXE. THE BOARDS WERE TRIMMED OR SHIMMED AT THE JOIST TO KEEP THE FLOOR LEVEL.

LOG JOIST

TONGUE AND GROOVE

SPLINE

SPLINED AND TONGUE-AND-GROOVE BOARDS TIE THE FLOOR TOGETHER FOR GREATER STRENGTH AND FOR LESS WARPING.

IN JAPAN, THE FLOOR MATERIAL DEFINES THE NATURE OF THE VARIOUS SPACES: EARTH OR STONE IN THE BARN AND ENTRANCE, WOOD IN THE KITCHEN AND WALKWAYS, AND TATAMI MATS IN THE LIVING AREAS. ROOM SIZES, AND SOMETIMES LAND AREAS,

STRAW TATAMI MAT (176 CM x 88 CM)

LIVING | KITCHEN | ENTRY

(TATAMIS) | (WOOD) |

| (STONE)

SECTION THROUGH A TRADITIONAL JAPANESE HOUSE

ARE MEASURED BY THE NUMBER OF TATAMI MATS HAVING AN EQUIVALENT AREA — FOR EXAMPLE, A SIX-MAT ROOM ACCOMODATES SIX TATAMI MATS.

The Chimney

MANY PRIMITIVE DWELLINGS HAVE NO OUTLET
SPECIFICALLY FOR THE SMOKE FROM THE FIRE. IN THE COMMUNAL
HOUSES OF THE WAURA INDIANS, THE SMOKE INSIDE
HELPS TO KEEP PESTS OUT, AND IT ALSO
PROTECTS THE THATCH FROM INSECTS
AS IT FILTERS OUT.

WAURA "MALOCA" (COMMUNAL HOUSE)
BRAZIL

PAN-P'O DWELLING, CHINA (4000 B.C.)
NOTE THE SMOKE HOLE AT
THE PEAK OF THE EARTH-
COVERED ROOF.

STONE SLAB
USED AS A RAIN HOOD OVER THE
SMOKE HOLE (ZUNI PUEBLO,
NEW MEXICO)

IN MANY PRIMITIVE
DWELLINGS AN OPENING IN THE ROOF ACTS AS
THE ENTRANCE, THE SOURCE OF LIGHT,
AND THE SMOKE HOLE.

HOUSE IN ANATOLIA,
TURKEY (6000 B.C.)

STONE SLAB HOOD OVER
SMOKE HOLE
ST. AUGUSTINE,
FLORIDA (CA. 1765)

SHORT CHIMNEY MADE
FROM OLD CLAY POTS
ZUNI PUEBLO,
NEW MEXICO

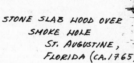

DURING THE LAST SEVERAL
CENTURIES THE FIREPLACE
AND THE ENCLOSED CHIM-
NEY HAVE REPLACED
THE FIRE PIT AND
THE SMOKE HOLE IN
MOST AREAS.

ADOBE FIRE-
PLACE AND CHIM-
NEY
NEW MEXICO
(CA. 1850)

THE FIREPLACE ITSELF IS
ALWAYS MADE OF SOME MINERAL
MATERIAL, BUT CHIMNEYS
HAVE BEEN BUILT WITH A
VARIETY OF MATERIALS.

THE LOG CHIMNEY'S
INTERIOR IS PLASTERED
WITH MORTAR TO PRO-
TECT IT FROM THE
HEAT OF THE FIRE.

LOG CHIMNEY
INDIANA (ca. 1850)

THIS LARGE WOODEN CHIMNEY
FORMS A FUNNEL-SHAPED HOOD
OVER A WALK-IN STONE
FIREPLACE.

SWITZERLAND

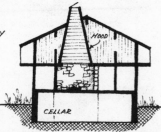

(SECTION THROUGH HOUSE)

VIRGINIA (18ᵗʰ CENTURY)

THIS BRICK CHIMNEY IS SET OUT
FROM THE WALL TO REDUCE THE
FIRE HAZARD AND THE HEAT INPUT
DURING SUMMER.

THIS MASSIVE
CHIMNEY SERVES A LARGE
FIRST-FLOOR AND A SMALL
UPSTAIRS FIREPLACE PLUS
A BAKE OVEN.

VIRGINIA (18ᵗʰ CENTURY)

COMBINED SMOKEHOUSE
AND SPRINGHOUSE WITH
A STAIRWAY BUILT INTO
THE CHIMNEY

CHESTER COUNTY
PENNSYLVANIA

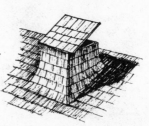

LIKE CURVED WALLS (SEE PAGE 125),
ROUND CHIMNEYS SAVE THE DIFFICULT
TASK OF MAKING CORNERS WHEN WORKING
WITH FLAT STONES, SUCH AS SLATE.

PLASTERED,
ROUND, STONE
CHIMNEY WITH
SLATE RAIN SHIELD
    (NORTHERN ENGLAND)

SHINGLED CHIMNEY
WITH RAIN HOOD (ALPS)

THIS CHIMNEY IS
INTEGRATED WITH THE
STUCCOED STONEWORK
OF THE HOUSE.

CHESTER COUNTY
PENNSYLVANIA

A SECTION TAKEN THROUGH THE
VAULTED HALLWAY OF THIS HOUSE SHOWS
HOW THE TWO FIREPLACE FLUES ARE
JOINED IN ONE CHIMNEY.

ASH LAWN, VIRGINIA
(DESIGNED BY THOMAS JEFFERSON)

The Doorway

The simplest doorways are simply holes in the wall, like this prehistoric door opening carved from a stone slab.

MALTA

Using tapered jambs can reduce the size of the stone lintel and can also make the opening appear taller

Mycenae, Greece (1325 B.C.)

The shapes of the openings below allow people to put their hands on the side and swing their legs over the high threshold and also permit someone to enter while carrying a wide load.

Mesakin dwelling, Sudan

Pueblo Bonito, New Mexico (11th century)

Narrow, recessed doors reduce the amount of sunlight entering and heating the interior.

Mykonos, Greece

Many African dwellings have small raised openings that minimize the passage of the sun's heat and also deter animals from crawling in.

Northern Cameroon

DOORS FOR SECURITY

MASSIVE WOOD DOOR
WITH HEAVY, METAL REIN-
FORCING PLATES AND
HINGES

TOWER OF LONDON
(CA. 1097)

AT THE ENTRANCE TO ITS NEST IN A
DRY BANK THE TRAP-DOOR SPIDER
CONSTRUCTS A SILK-HINGED DOOR
BY CEMENTING SOIL PARTICLES.
IT CLOSES UNDER ITS OWN
WEIGHT TO NEATLY COVER THE
NEST'S OPENING.

A PAIR OF HEAVY WOOD
DOORS ("PORTON") USED TO CLOSE
OFF THE PLAZA ("ZAGUAN") OF A
HACIENDA AND CONTAINING A
SMALLER, INSET DOOR, WHICH IS
USED MORE OFTEN

THE SMALL (4 FEET HIGH) MOTHER-IN-LAW
DOOR GIVES ACCESS TO AND FROM BOATS
IN THE CANALS.

AMSTERDAM

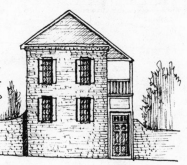

THE ANCIENT
PRACTICE OF ENTERING THE
HOUSE VIA A FULLY ENCLOSED
COURTYARD HAS REMAINED
POPULAR FOR CENTURIES
FOR REASONS OF SECURITY
AND PRIVACY.

CHARLESTON
SOUTH CAROLINA (19th CENTURY)

DOORWAY WITH PROTECTIVE
DECORATIVE GRILLE IN THE
TRANSOM OPENING, WHICH
PERMITS VENTILATION.

MORELOS, MEXICO

SLIDING, SLATTED FRAME
IN THE TRANSOM CAN BE LEFT
OPEN OR CLOSED.

JAPAN

THE TRADITIONAL DOOR IN JAPAN IS
A SLIDING PANEL. THE EXTERIOR ONES, OR
SHOJIS, ARE OF WOOD COVERED WITH
RICE PAPER, WHILE THE IN-
TERIOR ONES, OR FUSUMAS,
ARE OF WOOD COVERED
WITH A SOLID MATERIAL OR
CLOTH. ABOVE THE FUSUMA
IS OFTEN AN OPEN SPACE,
OR RAMMA (USUALLY HAVING
A DECORATIVE GRILLEWORK),
FOR VENTILATION.

RAMA

FUSUMA

LOUVERED DOORS
GIVE PRIVACY WHILE
ALLOWING GOOD VENTILATION,
AND THE TRANSOM WINDOW
LETS IN LIGHT AND/OR
FRESH AIR.

BERMUDA

DOORWAY WITH
WOOD LATTICE SCREEN IN
BOTH THE DOORS AND THE
TRANSOM FOR LIGHT
AND VENTILATION

VENEZUELA

DUTCH DOOR WITH BOTTOM CLOSED
TO KEEP ANIMALS OUT AND CHILDREN
IN AND WITH TOP OPEN FOR
LIGHT AND AIR

PENNSYLVANIA

SOLID LOWER
DOOR AND BI-FOLD
UPPER DOORS FOR A
DUTCH DOOR EFFECT,
PLUS A TRANSOM
WINDOW

GREECE

GRILLES ALLOW AIR AND VIEW THROUGH
THE DOORS, WHICH ENCLOSE
THE "ZAGUAN."

CALIFORNIA

THE SMALL GLASS
INSERTS IN THESE SHOJIS
CAN BE SLID OPEN FOR VEN-
TILATION OR CAN BE COVERED
BY SMALL SLIDING PANELS OF
TRANSLUCENT RICE PAPER FOR
PRIVACY. AS WINDOWS THEY
OFFER A NICE VIEW FOR
PEOPLE SEATED ON THE FLOOR.

JAPAN

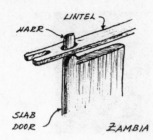

LINTEL

HARR

SLAB DOOR

ZAMBIA

THIS DOOR, MADE FROM A LARGE SLAB OF WOOD, HAS TWO PROJECTING LOBES, OR HARRS, WHICH ROTATE IN HOLES IN THE LINTEL AND THRESHOLD. THESE HARR-HUNG, OR PINTLE, DOORS WERE USED IN THE NEAR EAST MORE THAN 6,000 YEARS AGO.

LINTEL, OR "KAMOI," WITH ROUTED TRACKS FOR THE FUSUMAS

JAPAN

CLOTH USED FOR PRIVACY AND SHADING IN DOORWAY

APULIA, ITALY

DOORWAY WITH RAIN HOOD

BUCKS COUNTY PENNSYLVANIA (19ᵗʰ CENTURY)

PLAN OF DOORWAY SHOWING HOW THE DOUBLE DOORS FOLD AWAY INTO THE JAMBS

VISCHE, ITALY (15ᵗʰ CENTURY)

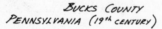

THE CORNER BRACES STIFFEN THE DOOR FRAME AND ALSO DEFINE THE ARCHED OPENING.

VASILOV, CZECHOSLOVAKIA (1839)

THE WINDOW

THE ANCESTOR OF THE WINDOW IS THE ANCIENT WIND EYE , AN OPENING IN THE ROOF THROUGH WHICH SMOKE COULD ESCAPE.

MUD AND THATCH HUT WITH WIND EYE
NORTHERN NIGERIA

ROOF WINDOW FOR LIGHT AND VENTILATION

TAKAYAMA, JAPAN

A VARIETY OF ROOF WINDOWS, OR DORMERS, EVOLVED TO BRING LIGHT AND AIR INTO THE LOFT SPACES.

HAMPSHIRE, ENGLAND

KENT, ENGLAND

HALF DORMER

SAINT AUGUSTINE, FLORIDA (18TH CENTURY)

DORMER WINDOW WITH A HIPPED ROOF

WILLIAMSBURG, VIRGINIA (1730)

DORMER WINDOW IN
A GAMBREL ROOF

WEST MEDFORD,
MASSACHUSETTS
(18ᵗʰ CENTURY)

DORMER WITH
LONG, CATSLIDE ROOF

EPHRATA,
PENNSYLVANIA

HIPPED GABLE ROOF WITH A
SMALL WINDOW IN THE GABLET
TO BRING LIGHT AND AIR
INTO THE LOFT

ENGLAND

EYEBROW WINDOWS
BRING LIGHT AND AIR TO UPPER
LEVEL WITHOUT REQUIRING A FULL-
HEIGHT WALL.

NEW HOPE,
PENNSYLVANIA

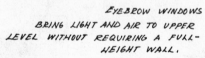

WINDOW

UPPER FLOOR

SUNLIGHT

STABLE BELOW

THE ANGLED BARN FLOOR ADMITS
LIGHT TO THE LOWER LEVEL FROM
WINDOWS ABOVE THE
FLOOR TIMBERS.

THE PUEBLO INDIANS
SOMETIMES MADE DIAGONAL HOLES AT
THE FLOOR/WALL JUNCTION TO ADMIT
LIGHT TO INTERIOR SPACES.

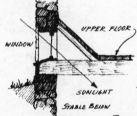

ZUNI PUEBLO, NEW MEXICO

BUILDERS DISCOVERED VERY QUICKLY
THAT WITH BEVELED JAMBS, A WINDOW OF WIDTH x
COULD ADMIT MUCH MORE SUNLIGHT (s) ENTERING
AT AN ANGLE.

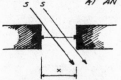 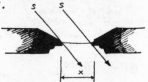

PRIMITIVE WINDOW WITH
SQUARED JAMBS

MEDIEVAL BEVELED WINDOW

RECESSED WINDOW
WITH ANGLED EXTERIOR
JAMBS AND LINTEL

ALPS

WINDOW WITH ANGLED
INTERIOR JAMBS AND SILL

NEW MEXICO

WEAVER'S WINDOW:

WINDOWS
HAVING ANGLED
STONE AND WOODEN FRAMES ADMIT EXTRA
LIGHT FOR WEAVING. ENGLAND (1600's)

BEVELED AND
VAULTED INTERIOR
WINDOW FRAME

PENNSYLVANIA

ANGLED JAMBS,
SCALLOPED AND VAULTED TOP,
AND DEEP SILL WITH SEATS

MICHOACAN,
MEXICO

CABIN WALL WITH THE
LOGS BEVELED AT THE WINDOW
TO ADMIT MORE LIGHT

SAVO PROVINCE, FINLAND

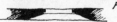

PLAN

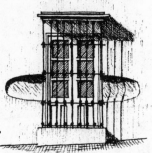

THE SCALLOPED
RECESSES IN THIS WALL
ALLOW A VIEW TO THE
SIDE FOR PEOPLE-WATCHING
FROM INSIDE.

ARCOS DE LA FRONTERA,
SPAIN

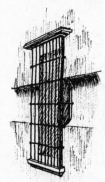

THIS RECESSED WALL BAND
ALLOWS A SIMILAR SIDEWAYS VIEW
THROUGH THE SMALL SECTION OF
GLASS AT THE SIDE OF
THE WINDOW.

SPAIN

METAL GRILLES
GIVE SECURITY
WHILE ADMITTING
LIGHT AND AIR.

GUANAJUATO,
MEXICO

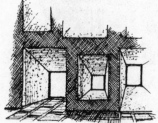

A VARIETY OF WINDOWS WITH
ANGLED JAMBS CREATE INTER-
ESTING LIGHT PATTERNS INSIDE
THIS CHAPEL.

CHAPEL AT RONCHAMP,
FRANCE

THE MOST COMMON DEVICE FOR
PROTECTING THE WINDOW FROM BOTH
WEATHER AND ATTACKERS
IS THE SHUTTER.

BOARD AND BATTEN SHUTTER
BERKS COUNTY,
PENNSYLVANIA

PANEL SHUTTERS
WITH DIAGONAL BOARD
BACKING

PEACH BOTTOM, PENNSYLVANIA

ARCHED PANEL SHUTTERS
COVERING A WINDOW THAT HAS A
VARIETY OF OPENING MODES

SIBERIA

SPLIT SHUTTERS FOR PARTIAL SHADING
ALONG WITH VENTILATION

DEADWOOD, SOUTH DAKOTA

LOUVERED
SLIDING SHUTTERS

NAGASAKI,
JAPAN

HORIZONTALLY HINGED
SHUTTER SET

KAVALLA,
GREECE

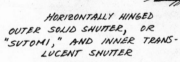

HORIZONTALLY HINGED
OUTER SOLID SHUTTER, OR
"SUTOMI," AND INNER TRANS-
LUCENT SHUTTER

JAPAN

145

INTERIOR SHUTTERS

A BARRED WINDOW
WITH INTERIOR PANEL
SHUTTERS REINFORCED
WITH A BOARD-AND-BATTEN
BACKING AND HAVING A
SMALL INSET DOOR,
OR WICKET, OUT OF
WHICH ONE CAN
PEEK.

SAINT AUGUSTINE, FLORIDA (18th CENTURY)

SECTIONED WINDOW
HAVING SMALL SHUTTERS WITHIN
THE LARGER, FULL-LENGTH,
INTERIOR SHUTTERS

MICHOACÁN, MEXICO

UPPER AND LOWER
BI-FOLD INTERIOR
SHUTTERS

CANTERBURY, NEW HAMPSHIRE
(1811)

SHUTTERS THAT
SLIDE VERTICALLY
FROM BELOW THE
WINDOW

CANTERBURY, NEW HAMPSHIRE
(1831)

DOUBLE SLIDING INDIAN
SHUTTERS, WHICH SLIDE
INTO THE WALL

WILMOT FLAT, NEW HAMPSHIRE
(19th CENTURY)

LOUVERED SHUTTERS
FOR SHADE,
PRIVACY, AND
VENTILATION

ITALY (14ᵗᴴ CENTURY)

PENNSYLVANIA
(19ᵗᴴ CENTURY)

LATTICEWORK IS WIDELY USED
IN WINDOWS AS A SUNSCREEN
AND TO GIVE SOME
PRIVACY.

WINDOW
WITH GRILLE
AND LATTICE

VENEZUELA

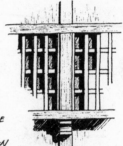

WINDOW WITH
AN ELABORATE WOOD LATTICE

KANAZAWA, JAPAN

THE JAPANESE SHOJI
SCREENS, WHICH ARE COVERED
WITH TRANSLUCENT RICE PAPER,
GIVE PRIVACY WHILE ADMITTING
NATURAL LIGHT.

SHOJI SCREEN
JAPAN

THE TRANSOM ABOVE THIS
WINDOW LETS IN SOME
LIGHT EVEN WHEN
THE SHUTTERS
ARE CLOSED.

HOLLAND

ENCLOSED BALCONY
WITH AWNING WINDOWS ON
THE FRONT AND CASEMENT
WINDOWS ON THE SIDES TO
ALLOW GREATER FLEXIBILITY
TO MEET DIFFERENT
WEATHER CONDITIONS

VALETTA, MALTA

THE UPPER SASH
OF THIS SECOND-
FLOOR WINDOW
PIVOTS FOR GOOD
AIR FLOW AND
EASY CLEANING.

CUMBRIA, ENGLAND

THE POINTED UPPER SASH
EXTENDS THIS DOUBLE HUNG
WINDOW UP INTO THE
TRIANGULAR ARCH.

CUMBRIA, ENGLAND

THIS TILTED
DOUBLE HUNG
WINDOW BRINGS
LIGHT IN THROUGH
THE SMALL WALL
AREA BETWEEN
THE ROOFS.

GRANTHAM,
NEW HAMPSHIRE

CORNER WINDOW
HOLLAND

COMBINATION OF WICKET (WINDOW WITHIN A WINDOW) AND CASEMENT WINDOWS WITH VERTICALLY AND HORIZONTALLY HINGED SHUTTERS

SWITZERLAND

THICK WALLS ALLOW THE WINDOWS TO BE RECESSED EITHER FROM THE OUTSIDE FOR WEATHER PROTECTION OR FROM THE INSIDE TO CREATE A SEAT OR A SHELF.

DEEP SILL WITH A WINDOW SEAT

PENNSYLVANIA

SILL SHELF

CZECHOSLOVAKIA

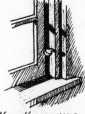

WINDOW TRACKS HELD ONLY WITH THUMBSCREWS ALLOW EASY REMOVAL OF SASH FOR CLEANING.

NEW HAMPSHIRE

A TRANSOM SIMPLIFIES THE BUILDING PROCESS BY PUTTING A DOOR AND A WINDOW UNDER ONE LINTEL.

NEW YORK

THIS SMALL WINDOW WAS PLACED IN THE ROOF TO BRING NATURAL LIGHT TO THE STAIRWAY AND HALL.

PENNSYLVANIA

THE STAIRWAY

SINCE PALEOLITHIC
TIMES SIMPLE STAIRWAYS
HAVE BEEN BUILT BY
CHOPPING A SERIES OF
NOTCHES INTO
LONG LOGS.

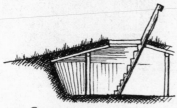

SALISH UNDERGROUND
TRIBAL BUILDING

CANADA

NORWEGIAN
LOG STAIR

TWIN NOTCHED LOGS
WITH STAIR TREADS
BETWEEN

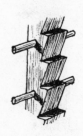

NOTCHED
TIMBER LADDER
WITH HAND RUNGS

PENNSYLVANIA

LASHED LADDER FOR
ROOF ENTRANCE
TO PUEBLO DWELLING

TAOS, NEW MEXICO

LADDER STAIR
WITH HANDRAIL

KANAZAWA, JAPAN

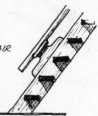

LADDER THAT
SWINGS DOWN FROM
BETWEEN CEILING
JOISTS

CANTERBURY,
NEW HAMPSHIRE

BUILDERS IN MANY
AREAS HAVE CHOSEN
TO PUT THE STAIRWAY
ON THE OUTSIDE OF
THE STRUCTURE TO
SAVE THE LIMITED
INTERIOR SPACE.

IRON AGE "CHIPURO" SHELTER
APULIA, ITALY

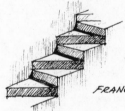

STONE HOUSE

LEMNOS, GREECE

STAIRWAY OF
STONES PROJECTING
FROM A MASONRY
WALL

SWITZERLAND

STEPS OF
CUT STONE BLOCKS

FRANCE

EXTERNAL STAIR-
WAYS ARE ESPECIALLY
POPULAR IN WARMER
CLIMATES.

INTERTWINING
NETWORK OF
STAIRWAYS

SPERLONGA, ITALY

THIS ARCHED
STAIRWAY HAS A
RAMP FOR PACK
DONKEYS BESIDE
STEPS FOR PEOPLE
AND LEADS UP
TO A TANK ROOM
ABOVE THE
CISTERNS.

GUANAJUATO, MEXICO

YEARS OF REPEATED WHITE-
WASHING GRADUALLY SOFTEN
THE SHARP ANGLE AT WHICH
WALL AND STEP MEET.

SIENA,
ITALY

STEPPED
PEDESTRIAN RAMP
ALONGSIDE A STAIRWAY
LEADING TO A BALCONY
CROSSWALK

MYKONOS,
GREECE

A STILE LETS PEOPLE
CROSS A FENCE BUT KEEPS LIVE-
STOCK IN, AND IT IS MUCH
EASIER TO USE THAN A GATE,
ESPECIALLY WHEN CARRYING
SOMETHING.

EPHRATA,
PENNSYLVANIA

ARCHED ADOBE
STAIRWAY WITH
STORAGE BELOW

SAN ANTONIO,
TEXAS
(19th CENTURY)

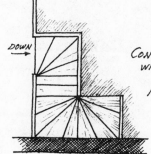

DOWN →

CONTEMPORARY SPIRAL STAIRWAY
WITH DOUBLE TURN

NEW LONDON, NEW HAMPSHIRE

SPIRAL STAIRWAY SCULPTED BY
WHARTON ESHRICK USING TENONED OAK
LOG TREADS AND DRIFTWOOD RAILINGS

PAOLI, PENNSYLVANIA

STAIRWAY WITH
STORAGE DRAWERS

RICHTERSWIL,
SWITZERLAND
(CA. 1756)

ENTRANCE TO
CONTEMPORARY HOUSE
BUILT OF MUD

UNITIZED ROOF
FOR EASY CONSTRUCTION
AND TRANSPORTATION
TO THE SITE

THIS STRUCTURAL ROOF PANEL
IS BUILT ON THE GROUND, BY
LASHING TOGETHER PALM LEAF RIBS,
AND THEN HOISTED UP
AND THATCHED.

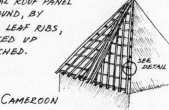

SEE DETAIL

DETAIL OF
LASHING

CAMEROON

IN TIMBER FRAMING,
WHOLE WALL SECTIONS,
OR BENTS, ARE
ASSEMBLED ON THE
GROUND, TILTED
INTO POSITION,
BRACED, AND THEN
FRAMED INTO THE
OTHER BENTS.

UNIONVILLE, PENNSYLVANIA

FORM BOARDS HAVE BEEN USED
OVER THE CENTURIES AS MOLDS FOR
BUILDING WALLS OF MUD, TABBY
(SEE PAGE 103), PACKED EARTH,
STONES (SEE PAGE 131), AND
CONCRETE.

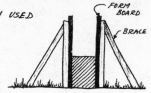

FORM BOARD
BRACE

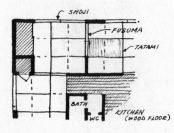

SHOJI
FUSUMA
TATAMI
BATH
WC
KITCHEN
(WOOD FLOOR)

IN TRADITIONAL JAPANESE
HOUSES, THE FLOOR PLAN, SHOJIS,
AND FUSUMAS ALL FOLLOW A
MODULAR GRID BASED ON THE
TATAMI MAT (SEE PAGE 132).

EXPANSION

THE INTUITIVE, CIRCULAR FORM OF THE NEOLITHIC BEEHIVE HUT (RIGHT) PRECLUDES THE SIMPLE EXPANSION OF THE INTERIOR SPACE,

BUT THE RATIONAL, RECTANGULAR FORM OFFERS THE POSSIBILITY OF EASY, LINEAR GROWTH (LEFT).

CARIB INDIAN STRUCTURE, GUIANA

ANOTHER WAY TO EXPAND A DWELLING IS TO BUILD ADDITIONAL UNITS THAT INTERFACE WITH THE EXISTING STRUCTURE.

HOUSE COMPOUND CAMEROON

VERTICAL GROWTH, AS IN THE TERMITE MOUND (ABOVE), IS ANOTHER EFFECTIVE MODE OF EXPANSION.

(CA. 1710)

(CA. 1750)

THE EARLY HOUSES OF ST. AUGUSTINE, FLORIDA WERE OFTEN EXPANDED VERTICALLY BY ADDING ANOTHER FLOOR ABOVE THE TABBY-WALLED FIRST FLOOR.

OTHER COMMON EXPANSION TECHNIQUES ARE THE LEAN-TO (LEFT) AND THE EL (RIGHT).

RHODE ISLAND

VERMONT

TEPEE COVER

TRAVOIS

THE TRAVOIS, DRAWN BY HORSES AFTER THEIR INTRODUCTION BY THE SPANISH, USUALLY CONSISTED OF TEPEE POLES BETWEEN WHICH THE TEPEE COVER (LEFT) WAS CARRIED WITH VARIOUS BELONGINGS.

THE WALL PANELS OF MANY YURTS COLLAPSE LIKE A SCISSORS GATE FOR EASY TRANS-PORTATION.

WALL OF MONGUL YURT

THE LARGE BEDOUIN TENTS ARE MADE TO BE EASILY CARRIED BY CAMELS.

THE BOW-TOP ENGLISH GYPSY VAN HAS PROVISIONS FOR SLEEPING, COOKING, EATING, AND SITTING WHILE TRAVELING, AND IT PROTECTS AGAINST BAD WEATHER.

PLAN OF GYPSY VAN

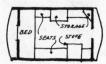

BED STORAGE SEATS STOVE

THE WOOD AND WATTLE-AND-DAUB SLEIGH HUTS OF THE BULGARIAN NOMADIC SHEPHERDS ARE LARGE ENOUGH TO HOUSE ENTIRE FAMILIES.

BULGARIAN SLEIGH HUT

BARGE
HOUSEBOAT

AMSTERDAM,
HOLLAND

WHETHER BECAUSE OF LIMITED AVAILABLE
LAND OR TOO HIGH A PRICE FOR IT, PEOPLE IN
MANY PARTS OF THE WORLD HAVE CHOSEN TO LIVE
ON THE WATER IN EVERYTHING FROM CONVERTED
BARGES TO DWELLINGS BUILT ON
ARTIFICIAL ISLANDS.

FLOATING
VILLAGE BUILT
ON A PLATFORM
OF BAMBOO

YELLOW RIVER, CHINA
(CA. 1668)

THE CHINESE EMPEROR WU-TI
(140 - 86 B.C.) HAD A FLOATING WOODEN
FORTRESS THAT MEASURED 600 FEET ON
A SIDE AND GARRISONED 2,000
MEN PLUS THEIR HORSES.

ALLEN, EDWARD. STONE SHELTERS. CAMBRIDGE, MA :
    MIT PRESS, 1969.

ANDERSON, CARDWELL. "PRIMITIVE SHELTER." AIA JOURNAL,
    OCT. AND NOV., 1961.

ARTHUR, ERIC, AND WITNEY, DUDLEY. THE BARN. GREENWICH,
    CT : NY GRAPHIC SOC. BOOKS, 1972.

BALDWIN, J., AND BRAND, STEWART. SOFT TECH. NEW YORK :
    PENGUIN BOOKS, 1978.

BEMIS, A.F., AND BURCHARD, J. THE EVOLVING HOUSE.
    CAMBRIDGE, MA : TECH PRESS, 1931.

BRODERICK, ALAN HAUGHTON. "GRASS ROOTS." LONDON :
    ARCHITECTURAL REVIEW 686 (FEB. 1954).

BUNTING, BAINBRIDGE. EARLY ARCHITECTURE IN NEW MEXICO.
    ALBUQUERQUE : U. OF N. MEXICO PRESS, 1976.

BUTTI, KEN, AND PERLIN, JOHN. A GOLDEN THREAD. PALO
    ALTO, CA : CHESHIRE BOOKS, 1980.

CAMESASCA, ETTORE. HISTORY OF THE HOUSE (1ST AMERICAN ED.).
    NY : PUTNAM, 1971.

CARVER, NORMAN F. JR. ITALIAN HILLTOWNS. KALAMAZOO, MI:
    DOCUMAN PRESS, 1979.

CHAMBERLAIN, SAMUEL. DOMESTIC ARCHITECTURE IN RURAL
    FRANCE. NY: ARCHITECTURAL BOOK PUBLISHING CO., INC., 1981.

CURRANT, WILLIAM, AND SCULLY, VINCENT. PUEBLO ARCHITECTURE
    OF THE SOUTHWEST. AUSTIN, TX : U. OF TEXAS PRESS, 1971.

DUPONT, JEAN-CLAUDE. HABITATION RURALE AU QUÉBEC. MON-
    TREAL : CAHIERS DU QUÉBEC / HURTUBISE HMH, 1978.

FITCH, JAMES MARSTON. AMERICAN BUILDING - 2 : THE ENVI-
    RONMENTAL FORCES THAT SHAPE IT. BOSTON: HOUGHTON
    MIFFLIN, 1972.

FITCH, JAMES MARSTON. "PRIMITIVE ARCHITECTURE." SCIENTIFIC
    AMERICAN, DEC. 1960.

FLETCHER, SIR BANNISTER. A HISTORY OF ARCHITECTURE ON THE
    COMPARATIVE METHOD. NY: CHARLES SCRIBNER'S SONS, 1963.

FOLEY, MARY MIX. THE AMERICAN HOUSE. NY: HARPER
    COLOPHON BOOKS, 1980.

VON FRISCH, KARL. ANIMAL ARCHITECTURE. NY: HARCOURT
    BRACE JOVANOVICH, 1974.

FUTAGAWA, YUKIO. VILLAGES AND TOWNS (VOLS. 1,3,5,6,8,9).
    TOKYO : ADA EDITA, 1973.

FUTAGAWA, YUKIO. WOODEN HOUSES NY : ABRAMS, 1979.

GARDI, RENÉ. INDIGENOUS AFRICAN ARCHITECTURE. NY :
    VAN NOSTRAND REINHOLD CO., 1973.

GARDINER, STEPHEN. EVOLUTION OF THE HOUSE. LONDON :
    CONSTABLE, 1975.

GASPARINI, GRAZIANO. LA CASA COLONIAL VENEZOLANA.
    CARACAS : U. CENTRAL DE VENEZUELA, 1962.

GAY, LARRY. *HEATING WITH WOOD*. CHARLOTTE, VT : GARDEN
    WAY PUBLISHING CO., 1974.
GIVONI, B. *MAN, CLIMATE AND ARCHITECTURE*. 2D ED. NY:
    VAN NOSTRAND REINHOLD, 1981.
GLASSIE, HENRY. *FOLK HOUSING IN MIDDLE VIRGINIA*.
    KNOXVILLE : U. OF TENNESSEE PRESS, 1975.
GRILLO, P.J. *WHAT IS DESIGN?* CHICAGO : U. OF CHICAGO
    PRESS, 1960.
GROPP, LOUIS. *48 ENERGY SAVING DESIGNS*. NY:
    PANTHEON, 1978.
GSCHWEND, FEHLMAN, AND HUNZIKER. *BALLENBERG: THE
    SWISS OPEN-AIR MUSEUM*. AARAU, SWITZERLAND: AT VERLAG, 1982.
HUBRECHT, R., AND DOYON, G. *L'ARCHITECTURE RURALE ET
    BOURGEOISE EN FRANCE*. PARIS: VINCENT, FREAL
    + CO, 1942.
KAHN, LLOYD (ED.). *SHELTER*. BOLINAS, CA: SHELTER
    PUBLICATIONS, 1973.
KAHN, LLOYD (ED.) *SHELTER II*. BOLINAS, CA : SHELTER
    PUBLICATIONS, 1978.
KENNEDY, ROBERT WOODS. *THE HOUSE AND THE ART OF ITS
    DESIGN*. NY: REINHOLD, 1953.
KINZEY, B.Y., AND SHARP, H.M. *ENVIRONMENTAL TECH-
    NOLOGIES IN ARCHITECTURE*. ENGLEWOOD CLIFFS, NJ:
    PRENTICE-HALL, INC., 1951.
KNOWLES, RALPH L. *ENERGY AND FORM*. CAMBRIDGE,
    MA : MIT PRESS, 1974.
KONSTANTINIDAS, N. ARIS. *ELEMENTS FOR SELF-KNOWLEDGE*.
    ATHENS : (PUBLISHED BY THE AUTHOR?), 1975.
MANUCY, ALBERT. *THE HOUSES OF ST. AUGUSTINE*, 1565-1821.
    TALLAHASSEE, FL: ROSE PRINTING CO., 1962.
MEANS, P.A. *ANCIENT CIVILIZATIONS OF THE ANDES*. NY:
    CHARLES SCRIBNER'S SONS, 1931.
MEGAS, ST. "STUDIES IN FOLK ARCHITECTURE." *LAOGRAPHIA*
    VOL. 26. ATHENS: SOCIETY OF HELLENIC LAOGRAPHY, 1969.
MERCER, ERIC. *ENGLISH VERNACULAR HOUSES*. LONDON :
    H.M. STATIONERY OFFICE, 1975.
MOHOLY-NAGY, SIBYL. *NATIVE GENIUS IN ANONYMOUS
    ARCHITECTURE*. NY: HORIZON PRESS, 1957.
MORGAN, LEWIS H. *HOUSES AND HOUSE LIFE OF THE AMERICAN
    ABORIGINES*. CHICAGO : U. OF CHICAGO PRESS, 1965.
MORSE, EDWARD S. *JAPANESE HOMES AND THEIR
    SURROUNDINGS*. NY: DOVER PUBLICATIONS, 1961.
OLGYAY, VICTOR. *DESIGN WITH CLIMATE*. PRINCETON :
    PRINCETON U. PRESS, 1963.
OLGYAY, ALADAR AND VICTOR. *SOLAR CONTROL AND
    SHADING DEVICES*. PRINCETON: PRINCETON U. PRESS, 1957.
OLIVER, PAUL. *SHELTER IN AFRICA*. NY: PRAEGER, 1971.
OLIVER, PAUL. *SHELTER, SIGN AND SYMBOL*. WOODSTOCK, NY:
    OVERLOOK PRESS, 1977.

PARKER, JOHN HENRY. *A Concise Glossary of Architecture*. LONDON: PARKE + CO., 1882.

PENOYRE, JOHN AND JAYNE. *Houses in the Landscape*. BOSTON: FABER AND FABER, 1978.

RAPOPORT, AMOS. *House, Form and Culture*. ENGLEWOOD CLIFFS, NJ: PRENTICE-HALL, 1969.

RAYMOND, ELEANOR. *Early Domestic Architecture of Pennsylvania*. NY: WM. HELBURN, INC., 1931.

RIVIÈRE, G. H. *Maisons de Bois*. PARIS: CENTRE GEORGES POMPIDOU, 1979.

ROBINSON, DAVID M. *Excavations at Olynthus: The Hellenic House*. BALTIMORE: JOHNS HOPKINS PRESS, 1938.

RUDOFSKY, BERNARD. *Architecture Without Architects*. NY: DOUBLEDAY + CO., INC., 1964.

RUDOFSKY, BERNARD. *Now I Lay Me Down to Eat*. NY: ANCHOR PRESS (DOUBLEDAY), 1980.

RUDOFSKY, BERNARD. *The Prodigious Builders*. NY: HARCOURT BRACE JOVANOVICH, 1977.

SAFDIE, MOSHE. *Form and Purpose*. BOSTON: HOUGHTON MIFFLIN, 1982.

SCHOENAUER, NORBERT. *6,000 Years of Housing* (VOL 1). NY: GARLAND STPM PRESS, 1981.

SERGEANT, JOHN. *Frank Lloyd Wright's Usonian Houses*. NY: WATSON-GUPTILL PUBLICATIONS, 1975.

SEVERIN, TIMOTHY. *Vanishing Primitive Man*. NY: AMERICAN HERITAGE PUBLISHING CO., 1973.

SHIPWAY, VERNA COOK AND WARREN. *The Mexican House: Old and New*. NY: ARCHITECTURAL BOOK PUBLISHING CO., 1960.

SKURKA, NORMA, AND NAAR, JOHN. *Design for a Limited Planet*. NY: BALLANTINE BOOKS, 1976.

SLOANE, ERIC. *An Age of Barns*. NY: BALLANTINE BOOKS, 1967.

SLOANE, ERIC. *A Reverence for Wood*. NY: FUNK AND WAGNALLS, 1965.

SPRIGG, JUNE. *By Shaker Hands*. NY: ALFRED A. KNOPF, INC., 1975.

WESLAGER, C. A. *The Log Cabin in America*. NEW BRUNSWICK, NJ: RUTGERS U. PRESS, 1969.

ZOOK, NICHOLAS. *Museum Villages of the U.S.A.* BARRE, MA: BARRE PUBLISHING, 1971.